LETTING GO OF SHOULD

LETTING GO OF SHOULD

MEGHAN SPEER

Meghan Speer

CONTENTS

Preface: 1

1   A Dead Fish and a Disastrous First Date   4

2   Whitney Houston Doesn't Belong Here, But I Do   9

3   I Am Not Campus Minister Material   17

4   Relationships: The Young One   24

5   A Quarter-Life Crisis   28

6   This Is NOT What Jesus Would Do   35

7   A God Kind of Errand   41

8   I Am Not the Axis   45

9   An Open Door   49

10   Taking the Red-Eye to a New Chapter   53

11   Toxic Fumes and Killer Tents   58

12   The Guilt of No   64

13   The Great Underpants Debate   68

14	Single to Single Mom	72
15	Well How About That, Brandon Heath!	77
16	One Step at a Time	84
17	Relationships: The Bad Boy	89
18	Outside the Little Boxes	94
19	Third Time is the Charm	99
20	Church Shopping	102
21	So I Sat for a Whole Year	109
22	Relationships: Whirlwind; Part One	114
23	Lessons From a Golf Course	118
24	Here, Have a Company	124
25	Me, Moses, and Jonah	130
26	A Cloud of Terror	134
27	I'm Not Dory. I Couldn't Keep Swimming	139
28	Paradise in a Pandemic	142
29	Relationships: Whirlwind; Part Two	146
30	Climbing Back Down	151
Acknowledgements		154

Preface:

Math is not my strong suit. It never has been. I could sit here and blame the failed "integrated math" approach to teaching that took over middle and high schools in the mid to late 1990s but the truth is I have a well-documented personal history that these issues started long before that. Friends and colleagues regularly refer to my calculations of things as "Meg Math." As in, not based on actual math at all.

Here's an example: Back in the summer of 2019 my business partner and I decided to host a grill party at the office one summer Friday afternoon. It was a simpler time then. A pre-pandemic time with no masks, where my hands weren't dried out from over sanitizing. One where our employees were allowed to be in the office and we could do fun things like sitting around a table together. On this particular day, we were grilling hotdogs and hamburgers. We had gotten through the main lunch rush and were talking about the second wave for our employees who worked an evening shift.

"Hey Meg, how much did we go through for lunch? Do we have enough for dinner?" he asked.

"We should have plenty. We only went through one box of burgers and thirty-two minus eight hot dogs so there's at least another box of each in the fridge," I replied.

He stopped. He looked at me with the face that he makes when I am not making much sense. "Hold up. Did you just say thirty-two minus eight hot dogs?"

"Yes," I said. "The package had thirty-two and we have eight left on a plate in the refrigerator."

"And thirty-two minus eight would be?" he asked.

"Twenty-eight. No, twenty-six? I think it's twenty-six. Or is it twenty-four?" I legitimately had no idea and was guessing at that point. Because math is not my strong suit.

There was never a point in my life where I thought "I should take a job as an accountant. I bet that would make me better at math." In fact, I knew all along in my very core that I shouldn't pursue any career that required decent math skills because it would only frustrate me and drain my energy by trying. But if you look closely at those last two sentences, you will see two words that carry way more weight than their letter-count would suggest.

Should and *Shouldn't*.

Our entire lives can be controlled by these two ideas if we let them. How many times a day do you find yourself thinking, "I should_____"? How many times have you thought, "I really shouldn't _____"? And how many times do you then NOT do the items on the should list, or do the items on the shouldn't list, and then get stuck in a guilt cycle over them? Stop the madness!

In my life I have been the victim of my own "should and shouldn't" lists more times than I can count. I've also let other people's lists of "should and shouldn't" define my choices far too often.

I told a dear friend that I was writing a book, she wanted to know why.

"What do you hope to get out of it?" she asked.

My answer was both huge and simple. "I hope that one person somewhere out there in the world reads this book and realizes that they are not the only person to struggle with expectations. I want this book to help one person realize that it's ok to change course even if that's scary. I hope that it helps one person see that whoever they are is amazing and they don't have to try to be anyone else to make other people happy."

In my life I have been the victim of my own "should and shouldn't" lists more times than I can count. I've also let other people's lists of "should and shouldn't" define my choices far too often.

So that's where this book starts. It looks at all the times that I have followed the *should* of my family, my friends, my colleagues, my church, and society. It's a story of the adventures that came from forging my own path every time a *should* didn't work out. It includes a few life lessons of times when *should* is actually wise. It is a journey of learning to trust myself and my life to a God who made me as a unique creation and has a plan better than any I could have imagined. It's a story of letting go so that I am able to reach for what's next.

CHAPTER 1

A Dead Fish and a Disastrous First Date

As I said, I hate math. And budgets, and reports, and most things analytical. I am not an operations person. I am a people person. All of my successes in the workplace for the last fifteen years have been in the following areas: sales, relationship building, mentoring, strategy and consulting, marketing and campaign design, creative work, and more relationship building. I score as an extrovert on every possible personality profile. For those who follow such things, I am a Meyers-Briggs ENFP and an Enneagram Type Two. This means that I am an extrovert who is very intuitive and reads people well, who also just loves to help. Are you seeing the people connection yet? It also means I am sometimes too nice for my own good and can avoid confrontation better than most. I am, by my very nature, a people pleaser. (See: Enneagram Two) It feels a lot easier for me to listen to other people and do what they want because I don't want to upset anyone or hurt any feelings.

This has been true for me for as long as I can remember. For most of my life, it has led me into situations where I followed a plan I didn't like or feel good about, just to avoid speaking my mind. This certainly reared its ugly head several times when I was growing up.

The first time my family went camping, I was six years old. I had very excitedly told my Granpap that were going camping and that we would be fishing at a little lake in the campground. Like the encouraging grandfather that he was, he told me to have a good time and bring him back a fish. We drove up to camp Friday night and Saturday was to be our fishing day. I was ready! My dad taught me and my little brother, who would have been four at the time, how to cast our lines and reel them in. My brother did it and pulled out a fish his first time around. Not to be outdone, I followed every last instruction but with no luck. He pulled fish after fish out of that lake and I couldn't even get a nibble. If that kept up, how would I possibly be able to bring Granpap a fish? I could not even think about disappointing him like that, so I moved a little further down the bank to try a new spot. I cast and reeled and cast and reeled but to no avail. I had nothing. Nothing, that is, until I spotted a fish lying in the dirty muck of the edge of the lake. The fish was on its last breath, having been stranded in the mud like that, but I didn't care. I also was not a kid who liked dirt, or anything slimy for that matter, but I did not care. In that moment, all I cared about was making sure I met Granpap's expectations, so I reached my little hand onto that goop, picked up that fish, and carried it over to my dad insisting that we take it home to show him. Even at six I couldn't stand the idea of disappointing someone.

This tendency to keep people happy reared its ugly head on one mortifying day in middle school too, when I agreed to go on a date with a boy – even though I knew I wasn't ready for dating – simply because my friends thought I should. This boy was very nice. He was very polite when he came with his mother to pick me up and take me to a movie. When his mom dropped us off at the theater, he grabbed my hand as we walked inside and every voice in my head was screaming, "If you run fast enough you can probably catch his mom and ask her to take you home. Run!" But I did not run. I went along inside, let him buy my movie ticket and some Junior Mints, and entered the theater. We were sitting there, waiting for the movie to start, and during a lull in the already awkward conversation, he leaned in to kiss me.

I had never kissed a boy before, and I wasn't too excited about the idea of joining the "girls who have kissed a boy" club. I was still nervous and, frankly, borderline panicked. So when I saw his face coming toward mine, I did the only thing I could think of. I started to cry.

Middle school boys are not known for their capacity for handling big emotions. Middle school girls, however, are chock-full of emotions and ready to explode with them at the drop of a hat. And this was much more than a hat. It was like that baseball at the beginning of the *Major League* movies that is wearing a hat and whizzes across the frame looking like it will jump off the screen and slam you in the face. Feeling like I was about to be struck in the face, not by a sloppy middle school first kiss, but by the actual hat-wearing baseball, immediately brought tears to my eyes. Then a new kind of panic overtook both of us when we simultaneously realized I was full-blown crying. Note: It is not good for anyone's self-esteem when the person they are trying to kiss starts to cry. I realized very quickly that my self-preservation mode had crushed this poor kid and I needed a new plan to try and save us both. Next came something I'm not proud of.

I lied. I used the fact that my beloved grandmother was in the hospital and not doing well as a scapegoat. Again, I'm not proud of it. But I needed some sort of explanation to get us out of the mess and "I'm so sorry! I went to see my grandma at the hospital this morning and she's not doing very well, and I'm just sad about it. I'm so sorry!" sounded way better in my stupid eighth grade brain than, "The idea of kissing you terrifies me so please keep your face away from mine." Honestly, there was no good way to get out of this scenario. Twenty-five years later, I still don't think I could come up with anything better. Except that now, what I do know, is that *better* would have been listening to myself from the beginning. A better plan would have been having the courage to say, "I'm not ready for all of this even though all my friends tell me I am" and not agreeing to the ill-fated date in the first place.

When you are young, it's easy to believe that everyone who is telling you what you should do is right, so you doubt your own instincts. If I could go back and tell my younger self anything, I would grab my shoulders and look square into my eyes and say, "Meghan your instincts are good. Follow them!" I am a firm believer that our world would be a very different place if we encouraged kids to develop and follow their instincts instead of writing out a detailed five-year plan. Maybe it would keep them from crying in movie theaters at thirteen-years-old in front of the terrified face of another thirteen-year-old.

Lesson learned: I should not make decisions based on anyone's timeline but my own.

CHAPTER 2

Whitney Houston Doesn't Belong Here, But I Do

All through high school my life revolved around choir, theater, speech and debate team, yearbook staff, and all things church youth group. My favorite classes were in English, writing, and public speaking and I knew I wanted to do something in those fields. When I was a junior in high school and began to look at colleges, I had no doubt in my mind what I wanted to do in college: a communications major with a performing arts minor. It's what all good theater kids do, right? Or at least all good theater kids who know that they don't want to pursue the arts as a career. I loved performing but I knew that cut-throat world wasn't something I wanted to take on for a lifetime.

My first college visit was with a friend of mine to see a school in Ohio that had a great communications major. She was a senior and very set on this particular school. I was a junior and just starting my search. The faculty member I met with asked me which area I'd like to concentrate my studies on and I didn't have an answer. Should I be a journalist? Or go into PR? Or maybe marketing? I had no clue. That professor told me I should think long and hard about that because if I went to school there, I would have to have an area of focus. The friend I'd gone to tour the school with told me that I should just say journalism next time someone asked so that I looked more prepared, so I went with it.

But journalism didn't feel right. I knew media professionals and I'd watched the way their lives were and I didn't think that was the pace or structure I wanted. When I was in middle and high school I used to babysit for a family in my church. The husband/father in that family was a local news anchor in Pittsburgh and I saw first-hand the long days, late hours, and weekends. I can still hear the panic in his voice when he called one night because a plane had crashed near the Pittsburgh airport and he needed to get out there immediately, but his wife wasn't home. My experience serving as the on-call babysitter to someone in journalism was as close as I wanted to get to that field. The hard part was that I didn't know what I did want and my friend and the professor both seemed pretty sure they knew what I should do, so I started telling people I was thinking about journalism. My stomach turned every time I said it.

As I mentioned, I was very active in my high school's Speech and Debate team. To clarify, I was a very active member of the speech side of that team. Debate, while I did it a few times, was not my favorite. I was already giving up a perfectly good Saturday to compete and now they wanted me to intentionally spend it arguing with people? I didn't think so. But when it came to things like Dramatic Interpretation or Duet Acting, I was in my element. So much so that I was willing to be on a school bus by 7:30 a.m., in dresses and heels, almost every Saturday morning October through April for four years, heading to schools all over the area. Or giving up whole weekends to go compete across the state. A thing I never really understood was that this team was called the Forensics team. We competed in National Forensics League events locally and across the country. It had nothing to do with the investigation of deceased persons, so I was not sure where the name came from, but there it was. The thing is, in the late 1990s all those crime drama shows were not yet commonplace. All of the shows that made forensic work known to the masses had not come out, so I didn't even know the breadth of that field.

Apparently on some college interest form or another, I had written that I was involved in forensics so when I received a letter from a college, inviting me to a special visit day on campus just for people interested in forensics, I was very excited. I hadn't really given much thought to competing in college, but if they were having a whole day about it, I figured it was worth looking at. As my dad and I walked into the room for the first scheduled activity on the list it became very clear, very quickly, that there had been some kind of error. The first table that was set up in the university's gymnasium for this event had crime scene photos that I'm pretty sure you wouldn't be able to show on network television. I looked at the table, horrified by what I saw. My dad looked at the table with an equal mix of horror over the situation and confusion because he knows me well enough to know that this was certainly not for me. We didn't even make it to the second table. We gave the table one more glance, looked at each other and wordlessly exited the building. While I didn't really have an interest in competing in speech competitions after high school, I really had no interest in pursuing a career in the medical examination field. When we got to the car we both laughed uncontrollably at the mix up, went and got some lunch, and crossed that school right off my list.

Determined not to make the same mistake again, I signed up to go to a personal visit day at the next school on my list. Never again would I be sucked into the mess of a planned day, I decided, so off my dad and I went to a small liberal arts school in northwestern Pennsylvania. It was the quintessential East Coast Liberal Arts school campus; beautiful old brick buildings, tree-lined walkways, and '90s kids in baggy jeans and flannel shirts playing hackysack outside the student union. When I toured this school, where I would end up attending, the head of the department started her well-rehearsed chat with me with this sentence: "Our communications program is different from other schools in that we don't have a specific focus. Instead, our program is based on communication theory and all the ways that communication happens. It's a firm foundation you can build on in any communications career you choose." Sold! I was hooked. Yes, the campus was lovely and I loved the feel of the school, but mostly I loved that I didn't have to know what I wanted to do yet. I loved that this program would give me options in the field I was set on.

On my second visit to that school, I learned another lesson on my life list of *shoulds*. As in, one should always ask for more information and clarity if one wants to put her best foot forward.

I went to campus that day to audition for the college choir director. Among his many directing and teaching duties, he was also responsible for adjudicating the incoming freshman choir scholarship. I had been singing in choirs for years and fully planned to do that in college, so I was excited to learn there was a potential scholarship for it! What I didn't know: this school has a long, rich tradition of Lutheran choral music. As in, a lot of beautiful rich harmonies and intricate parts, mostly done a capella or with giant pipe organs, and most of all fairly serious pieces of music. I had grown up singing show tunes and Dixieland jazz. The closest I'd come to serious was the version of Handel's *Hallelujah Chorus* our high school choir sang at the end of every holiday concert. I was woefully unprepared to audition against students who had done the research about the college's choir program and who came prepared with Italian arias and French art songs, and things in actual Latin. I, on the other hand, auditioned with Whitney's Houston's "One Moment in Time."

When I walked into the audition room, the director was as kind as could be. He ran me through scales and vocal range exercises to see where I would land. He seemed duly impressed with my range, especially my high soprano notes, so I felt like it was all going very well. Then I handed him the sheet music for "One Moment in Time," which was the song I had been practicing to sing at a senior banquet that year. I really liked how my voice sounded and the emotion I could convey in it. While I'm no Whitney, I was feeling pretty pleased with myself over it. When I handed him the sheet music he looked confused.

"One Moment in Time," he said. "I don't think I know this one."

"It's a great ballad," I replied.

"It appears to be in English."

"Yes, sir."

"Interesting. Is it a pop song?"

"Yes, sir. By Whitney Houston."

"Interesting. Ok, well, let's see how it goes."

I could tell right away that "interesting" did not mean "great." He began to play the introduction to the piece and I came in nice and clear to sing through the first verse and the first chorus before he stopped me.

"Miss Speer, that was fine. Thank you," he said, in a tone of relative apathy.

"I'm sorry. Do you want me to try it again?"

"No. But I'd like you to listen to something."

He walked over and put a CD in the stereo and played a track of the most beautiful a capella piece. It was in Italian and had soaring soprano and tenor notes on top of booming basses and bright alto lines. It was the kind of music that, when you hear it live, lingers in the rafters for a moment before anyone dares to applaud.

"That, Miss Speer, was our choir last year on their spring tour home concert. That is the type of music we do here. You certainly have the top range to do very well with that, but the song you picked didn't showcase that nor did it match the style of the work we do. I'd be happy to have you in the choir, but I don't think the scholarship is the right fit for you this season. Maybe next year."

Through the course of my college career, that same director taught me more about music, theory, and technique than I could have ever hoped to have learned in a lifetime, but more importantly he taught me about life. From the moment of that first audition and all the way through my senior recital, he and his wife were a huge influence in shaping me as a vocalist and as a human. Since then, I have been prepared for every audition I have ever gone to. I have over prepared for meetings and sales pitches. I have always asked enough questions to make sure I am ready, and I have him to thank for that. Well, him and Whitney Houston, I suppose.

Even without the choir scholarship, I went to that school as a communications major and I loved learning about rhetorical theory, business communications, interpersonal communications, and yes, even mass media communications. I'm sure the professor at the first school I visited meant well. I know my friend had good intentions. But the professor wanted me to pick his college and so his *should* was motivated by enrollment numbers. My friend was, and is, a brilliant over-achiever. I know her *should* was from a place of wanting the best for me (and maybe a little because she wanted us to go to school together). I'll be honest and tell you I almost listened, even though I knew in my gut that journalism wasn't my answer, because I wanted to make them happy. I knew that their *shoulds* were a *should not* for me. Listening to myself as I was trying to figure out my college plans, choosing what I wanted instead of what outside influences wanted, was the first time I remember trusting my gut enough to pick my own path.

Lesson learned: I should take the reins in my own decision-making and I should always, always do the research and be prepared.

CHAPTER 3

I Am Not Campus Minister Material

The thing no one told me about a theoretical-based communication major is that when you are graduating and starting to look for entry level jobs, none of the job postings say "communication theorist." I loved my courses and the experiences I had from day one, in and out of the classroom. I pledged a sorority, sang in two choirs, lived in the theater, worked on the newspaper, participated in student government, and worked with the campus Christian fellowship group. I loved everything about my college experience at this picturesque small liberal arts school. I knew I had picked the right school for me.

I started learning lessons there even on day one. Another example of a *should not*. As in, one should not go across campus by themselves on the first night at a new school as a super innocent eighteen-year-old girl because some frat guy that she met on AOL Instant Messenger told her to. Honestly, if any of the youth group kids I worked with told me this story, I would have yelled at them for being so careless. But live and learn, I suppose.

The summer after I graduated from high school, I did what all good '90s kids did to communicate: I changed my AIM profile to include the school I was heading for in the fall. Back before the days of Facebook and Twitter, AOL Instant Messenger reigned supreme as the way to connect with friends old and new, as well as the only option we had for leaving status messages so everyone knew just how busy or emotional you were on that given day. The perfect "away message" crafted with just the right font and color combination was a thing of beauty and it was our first foray into digital connections. Once I had updated my profile appropriately, I then searched other people who had the school in their profiles and started to chat with them to make some connections. One guy I "met" was going to be a junior that year. He seemed nice enough online and we had some good conversations over the summer. He had some good insights into college life and some very funny stories about his fraternity brothers and at the time, I didn't know much about fraternities or their reputations. I was super naïve.

The last message he sent me said that he was heading to school the next day because he was helping with freshman move-in day and the orientation theater show, so he wouldn't be online as much, but to call the operator when I got to campus and ask for his extension and give him a call so we could hang out in person. Yes, I am that old. We didn't readily have internet access in our dorm rooms and each student's landline extension was a useful piece of information. We relied heavily on a well-crafted system of messages left on dry-erase boards hung on doors because cell-

phones were still mostly in bags and only for very important people. That's all beside the point. The point is, I did exactly what
he said to do. After all the orientation day festivities were over for
the night, I called the operator who nicely told me the guy's extension. He answered when I called and said he and a few of his
brothers were all on the floor of the dorm they lived in and that
I should come over and hang out with them. And I WENT. I
left my roommate and new-found floor friends behind, ventured
out across the campus by myself, climbed to the third floor, and
knocked on his door. To this day, this might be the bravest (or
most reckless) thing I have ever done in my life.

Thankfully, the guy was as nice as he'd seemed online and
the guys of that fraternity became my favorite group to hang out
with. I'm still friends with many of them to this day. But the out-
come doesn't change the fact that, especially nowadays, it is un-
wise to go visit random men from the internet without telling
anybody else about your whereabouts.

Throughout my time in college, I could see my tendency for
leadership emerging more and more each semester. I had gone
from just being in a lot of clubs and organizations to being a
part of the leadership for all of them. I was no longer just in two
choirs, I was also choir president. I was on the officer board for
my sorority. I was an officer for the theater group, on student
government, and on the editorial board for the newspaper. I'll
be honest, I was feeling pretty smug about all those accomplish-
ments, which is what led me to one leadership lesson I carry with
me to this day: People matter more than position.

My junior year, when student government association (SGA)
elections rolled around, I joined up with some friends who had

also been active in SGA, as well as on the paper with me, to make a whole ticket of officers. That ticket was running in opposition to the slate of officers who had run SGA last year and was looking for a second term and that slate of officers included one of my sorority sisters. I was the only female on the slate with my friends, almost feeling like a token, but I took that as a source of pride. I was feeling pretty good about asking to be included so I wholeheartedly bought into their idea and vision for what they wanted to see SGA accomplish. That buy-in also meant that I was giving my support to the ways that those guys went after the current officers. Some of their quotes on college radio interviews, the things they said in the paper, or the posters they created were harsh and even borderline hurtful, but my existence on their ticket backed those actions even if my quotes had a different tone. This election, silly now as I look at it in the grand scheme of life, tore at relationships I held with friends and sisters. I put ambition over those relationships. I sold out my values of caring for people for the promise of a position. In the end, my crew lost that election and the previous group remained in leadership. I remember sitting on a cold, stone bench outside of my dorm when results were announced. It was one of those gray western Pennsylvania days where you just wish it would snow because then at least the cold would be worth it, and it matched my mood. I knew that day that I hadn't handled things well. I knew I owed my sisters an apology and while they were gracious, some of those relationships never went back to what they were because I had chosen to value a potential position over those people. To this day, I try and remember that day on a cold bench whenever an opportunity presents itself. "Who will be affected and how can I mitigate that?" is a filter I still run things through when it comes to leadership choices, because people have to matter.

In the spring of 2002, with graduation looming on the horizon, I had a panicked realization one morning: Trusting my gut and picking this school with its "firm foundation of communication" meant I had no clear career path. I was so focused on the goal of "communication major with a performing arts minor" that I had failed to see that all I had done was kick the can of "what do you want to be when you grow up" down the road by four years. I was floored! I had not seen this coming.

Suddenly all the confidence I had felt from my decision to come to this school and mastering the college life for the last four years vanished in an instant that morning as I sat at breakfast listening to other seniors talk about their plans after graduation. I had never felt so woefully behind. I started asking anyone who would listen what they thought I should do. Everyone, that is, with two notable exceptions: myself and God. I asked my parents and my friends and my professors. I rehashed it with my roommate enough times that I'm pretty sure she wanted to punch me by mid-terms. I was scrambling to find anyone with an answer. Everyone had a different opinion. I got everything from "you should go to grad school," to "you should look at ministry jobs," to "you should apply for every entry-level marketing job you can find and see what sticks."

One of those conversations led me to a discussion with a family friend from the church where I grew up. He was the head of a nonprofit ministry to college students and he encouraged me to apply for their staff positions. That discussion led me to going to their spring staff retreat and interviewing with their head of recruitment. I was accepted to the program and began the process of interviewing for open positions that would have had me working with a local church to help with youth ministry and also with the college or university close to that church to lead campus ministry. I interviewed with three of those churches and was offered positions with each one of them. On one hand I was thrilled. Graduation was fast approaching, and I finally felt like I had something to say when someone asked me what was next. "It looks like I'll be going into campus and student ministry," I would say. Then the asker would inevitably say, "Wow, good for you! That will be so rewarding!' I'd smile, and thank them, and try to pretend like this was my plan all along.

It was not my plan. I never had a plan. When I graduated in May of 2002, I did so as the senior class speaker. I sang a solo at the Baccalaureate service beforehand. It was the last day of a life I was great at. I went home single and jobless to try and figure out what came next.

What came next was a move that confused and frustrated a lot of people in my life. I turned down all three ministry job offers within a week of moving back home. No one seemed to understand. Everyone around me seemed to think that turning down multiple job offers when I didn't have another plan was "crazy" and "irresponsible." I didn't know what I wanted to do, but I knew that I got that same stomach-churning feeling that talking about being a journalism major used to give me back in high school every time I said I was going into college ministry. I just couldn't do it. It was one of those times when I could feel proud about the fact that I didn't follow everyone else's advice. As a side note, I now go to church with the man who was my liaison to the college ministry, the one who then had the job of going back to three places to tell them I'd said no. We've only spoken of this once and he really is the kindest man. But deep down I kind of believe he still thinks I'm the worst. But that also may be my people-pleaser-based guilt talking.

Lesson learned: I don't have to have a plan ready just because everyone else around me does or because of some arbitrary deadline like "graduating."

CHAPTER 4

Relationships: The Young One

If you were to ask me when I was in middle or high school what kind of life I'd be living when I was forty, I would have told you some version of "I'll be married with a few kids." I just assumed that this is how life was supposed to unfold for everyone. I grew up in the northern suburbs of Pittsburgh and every adult I knew was living some form of this life. It never occurred to me that said life situation would not be handed out like pizza bagel samples at Costco. Believing this fallacy has led to a lot of *should-nots* in my relationships. I got stuck in this idea that being married with kids was the way someone like me should live. What I now see is a pattern in my dating life that falls into *should not*. It's funny to see how some of my most ill-fated relationships have mirrored other things that were happening in my life, and my second semester–senior year boyfriend from the second semester of my senior year was no exception.

When I was in college I was in both choir and chamber singers. Every spring these groups loaded up a giant tour bus and hit the road to do ten to twelve concerts in the ten days of Spring Break. My freshman year we did a run through the Carolinas and Georgia. Sophomore year was a more local Pennsylvania and West Virginia tour, as we were headed for a large European tour that summer. My junior year was a legendary Florida tour. My senior year we did the New York, New Jersey, and Delaware run. It was on that senior year tour that a *shouldn't* have boy appeared.

I was already feeling like I was behind the eight ball because I didn't know what I wanted to be when I grew up. To add insult to injury, classmates were getting engaged left and right and I wasn't even dating. It felt like I was failing all over the place at creating this life I should have had! Enter a cute, naïve freshman tenor.

We had a whirlwind romance on that tour – snuggling on the bus during long stretches of driving, having our first kiss at the top of the Empire State Building on our one night off, and taking turns going on soup and ginger ale runs when we both inevitably came down with the crud that seemed to happen to everyone after returning from tour. It had been over a year since I had dated anyone seriously and it was lovely to do that thing where you walk out of a class and find someone is waiting there to walk you to lunch. I am only slightly embarrassed to tell you how often we reenacted scenes from *Moulin Rouge*.

Back in college, a very dear friend and I had developed a bit of a routine. He went to a college about thirty minutes from mine and whenever one of us started dating someone, we met halfway between our campuses at a local chain diner so that we could introduce said new significant other to said dear friend so that we could make sure the other hadn't chosen poorly. It says a lot about both of our dating records that such a quality assurance process had been put into place. A week or two after arriving back to campus from tour, I loaded my newly found paramour in my car and we headed to the diner. About forty-five minutes into our meal, when said paramour had excused himself to the restroom, my friend looked at me and said, "Meg. Are you kidding me? He's so young. Nice kid but, wow, so young. Are you sure this is a good idea?" He immediately nicknamed him Junior. He still makes fun of me for Junior to this day.

Junior and I dated for a month or so after tour, but as April was wrapping up and finals loomed, so came the realization that I was leaving and he still had years of school ahead of him. He was very sweet but firm in saying that he didn't see this going long term and so ending it seemed like the best bet. I tried my hardest to cling to it and make him see that it could work. Not because I actually loved him or thought it could, but because in my head I simply could not imagine graduating from college with neither firm job plans nor any relationship to speak of. I felt like an utter failure! I was so caught up in making sure that my life looked how I thought everyone expected it to look that I was willing to ignore the fact that Junior and I had nothing in common outside of the fact that we both had high vocal ranges for our particular gender and were good at using those voices to sing in harmony with other people. .I know now that the pressure of "*should*" can often lead to actions that "should not" have been taken.

Lesson learned: I can't force myself, or other people, to feel something that isn't there.

CHAPTER 5

A Quarter-Life Crisis

On the second anniversary of September 11, I had a mental breakdown. It had nothing to do with the events of September 11, 2001 at all, but it's just one of those dates that will always stick in your head. After graduating from college and moving home I did my best to find a job that was not in the ministry field. I interviewed for a few things and got offered a few things, but none of them felt right for some reason. I was still hell-bent on trusting my gut. My gut said those weren't the answers. Eventually, I saw a job posting to be the communications assistant for a kids' play program. This particular company held classes for moms and their kids under five in various areas of physical fitness and music. The position would be assisting the owner of the franchise with things like marketing, booking classes, and responding to people who were interested in those events. As it turned out, I would also be helping to teach some of the classes. For a moment that seemed like the ideal plan: A job that would get me into a communications field and still let me use a little bit of that performing arts background I was so committed to.

I started the job in the late summer of 2002. Within a few months I was determined that it was time to trade in my college car and get something for myself that looked like it fit the professional I saw myself becoming. I went out and signed a lease on an adorable, brand-new blue Volkswagen Jetta. I ignored everyone who said I should just buy a used car and rolled my eyes at their commonsense statements about depreciation. For a while I was very pleased with myself. I had a job, I had a cute little car, and everything was getting back on track. But then I got it in my head that somebody who has graduated from college and started a job and has a cute little car should certainly not be living at home. There was that *should* again. I felt like everybody wanted to know why I was still at my parents' house and not yet out on my own, so I started apartment hunting. Part of me knew I wasn't ready. Part of me knew that it just didn't feel right. But I went anyway and signed a lease on a very tiny studio with only one electrical socket in the main living room. Because at 22 you don't know any better. I did it because at that point in my life, all I knew is what other people thought I should do.

I should have seen this breakdown coming. I was excellent at being in school. Not always excellent AT school mind you, but at the process of it. From kindergarten through twelfth grade and through all four years of college, I did well in the structure and the system of it. I loved being a part of activities way more than I loved being a part of classes, but either way, I liked the structure of feeling a part of something. I liked the fact that there was a feedback system in place to tell me how great I was doing. Teachers generally liked me and told my parents how sweet I was. At my small college my professors became friends. I thrived in that system.

As it turned out, the real world had no such system. I had a job that seemed to be going well, I was spending hours each week volunteering with the church youth groups and running Bible studies, and nobody seemed to want to pat me on the back for all of my effort. I didn't understand this lack of system and it rocked me to my core. Clearly what I was doing wasn't enough to be noticed by society's standards, so I had to figure out how to play the game. I was not mentally or financially prepared to move out. I should have given myself time to adjust to life in the real world. I should have listened to my parents who didn't think this was a good idea. There were a lot of *shoulds* in this scenario.

I moved into that apartment, almost one year to the day after starting my job, as a way to prove to myself that I knew what was best. I was very wrong. On one hand, it taught me some valuable life lessons. Like, you should always make sure that any apartment you rent has more than three electrical outlets, for example. One in the kitchen, one in the bathroom, and one in the main living area may seem fine at first, but it makes having any light or clocks or phone chargers in the bedroom a tricky challenge.

Within a few weeks, I noticed the financial stress wearing on my health. A few weeks after that, I became paranoid about someone watching me. On that September 11 morning, I got in the shower to get ready for work, put *body wash* in my *hair*, and then melted down over the fact that I didn't even know how to shower anymore. The last thing I remembered that day was calling my parents' house in a fit of tears. The next week was a giant blur. I think I slept through most of it. I knew there were doctors' appointments and a therapist visit. Somehow, I got out of my lease and all my things got back to my parents' house, but I have no recollection of how either thing happened. I left my job or got fired from it, I'm still not sure. I lived in that blur for a month. There is still so much of that time period that I don't remember. In fact, if I'm honest, most days I try to forget that it ever happened. I knew that people were disappointed in me, I'm sure I was disappointed in myself. It was not a period of time I liked to dwell on, and yet the fact that it happened shaped me in ways I'm thankful for.

Five weeks post meltdown, with the last of the paychecks from my first job having already come in as well as the next bill for my cute car, I realized that hiding on my parents' couch with no sources of income was not a sustainable solution. I knew that mentally and physically I was in no shape to do anything serious, but I had to do something. I went and applied for a cashier's job at Target. For the first three months of that job I showed up, scanned people's items for six hours and went home. It was mindless and I was fine with that. It gave me enough money to cover my car payment, and really that was the only goal at the time. I was twenty-three and pretty well convinced that I had peaked in college and that life was all downhill from there.

A year later, by the fall of 2004, I had moved into a full-time employee position with the Target Corporation. I had fully mastered all aspects of front-end life. I could cashier, I could work the guest service counter, I could even run the food court. I did my full forty hours a week. I was also doing about fifteen to twenty hours a week at my church. I had taken a part time job running children's ministry programs and summer camp and had also gone back to helping with youth group. Anytime I ran into someone from high school or college at a bar or party, I'd talk about the church part, ignoring the fact that it was only part time and not mentioning the Target gig all together. I was feeling badly enough about myself without having to admit out loud that I was single, living at home, and a cashier. My peers were all working their way up at cool tech startups, or finishing law school, or getting married, and I felt like a giant failure every time I talked to them. Everyone else was winning at this game of life and I couldn't keep up. I kept thinking I should be more, should do more, should have found love by now, and should have taken a different path. The weight of all that *should* was crushing me.

I felt stuck. I didn't know how to get out. And then a weird thing changed my perspective. On a slow day at Target, one of the store managers asked me if I would do a project for him. It sounded better than standing around doing nothing, so I followed him down the main aisle. If you have been to a Target, or to any general retailer for that matter, you have likely seen the wall of travel-sized things. Mini versions of everything from shower supplies to laundry detergent in wire baskets. This wall is the nightmare of every retail worker because it is always a mess. On this particular day, we were getting ready for a visit from the district manager and the travel-sized wall was a disaster area. I was tasked with solving the problem. It had been a solid sixteen months since anyone had tasked me with solving any problem outside of "what songs should we sing at youth group this week" and I was a little surprised at the sense of pride I took in it. Three hours later, the wall was absolute perfection. Not one item was in the wrong bin and two shopping carts full of items that never belonged on the wall in the first place were ready to be put back in their rightful places. I was extremely pleased with myself. More importantly, this manager was very pleased with me. It felt good.

A month or two after that, that same manager recommended me for a promotion and I took the leap and interviewed. Much to my surprise, I got the job and was given a section of the store over which I was responsible. It felt good. I started hanging out with other people from work and having new friends felt good. The only thing that didn't feel good was church. Well, that and the fact that I was regularly getting made fun of for my Target walkie-talkie etiquette.

"Hey Meghan, what's your location?" one of my coworkers asked over the walkie.

I looked around and, wanting to give as accurate a description as possible, I replied "I'm in men's pants."

I could hear giggles coming from all over the store, not just from other employees with walkie-talkies on their belts, but from any customer within hearing range.

"Meghan, please leave what you do in your own time off of the company communication channels," came the voice of my boss. I was mortified. I wish I could tell you that was the only time I said the wrong thing by walkie. It was not. I had a bad habit of speaking before I thought and sometimes what I said sounded a lot dirtier than I intended. Unfortunately, the more I seemed to find my feet again at work, the worse that church felt.other things felt. Like church. Church had always been my place and my community but in that season, it felt less and less like a place I belonged. My peers were getting married and starting families, and I wasn't. So many of the people there had known me since I was nine years old and it felt like they still expected the kid they knew instead of the adult I was becoming, even if that adult didn't fit the traditional norms. In that season the Church as a whole wasn't doing a great job of talking about mental health struggles either, which made me feel even more like an outsider. Work turned into a place where people saw me as a leader and appreciated what I brought to the table. It became a place where people didn't judge struggles and worked as a team and that was the opposite of what I was finding in my church.

Lesson learned: I shouldn't let the opinion of others and their yardsticks for success define my plans or my self-worth.

CHAPTER 6

This Is NOT What Jesus Would Do

My family has always been a faith-based one. Growing up, both of my parents were heavily involved in the churches we attended. They led Bible studies and Sunday school classes, directed children's musicals and Christmas pageants, served as choir directors and led worship. My parents had been a part of small groups and my dad was usually an elder. I followed suit. I was in the children's pageants, I was in a youth group and a small group, worked in the nursery, and helped with summer camp. I even spent a few years in the puppet ministry and went to puppet ministry competitions. I was DEEP into the 1990s WWJD purity culture vibe of the evangelical church on top of all my school activities. Honestly, it took me a long time (as in most of my 30s) to realize that Philippians 4:13 was not meant as a mandate to continually add more church activities to your hectic schedule so that you can proudly boast in how much God is giving you the strength to do all the things. Don't get me wrong. It was a fun way to grow up and I made some of my dearest lifelong friends in that church. I wouldn't trade those days for anything, but I wish I'd learned more about what scripture really taught and what it means to really follow Jesus in the midst of all the *McGee and Me* videos and DC Talk albums.

When I took the job at the same church I had grown up in, I was excited to help a new generation of kids have those experiences. The thing is, when you work forty plus hours per week, with a lot of weekends, help run two youth groups and an elementary group, and oversee Sunday school for grades one through five, it keeps you pretty busy. To burn off some stress, I was regularly hanging out with my work friends who were not so into the church culture. It felt like I was living two lives. I'd work a Saturday closing shift, leave work at 11:00, and go with my friends to the bar. We'd party, and sometimes after party, and then I'd crash for a few hours before showing up at church to run the aforementioned Sunday school programs while trying my best to not reveal that I was hungover. I was usually successful. I was smoking, both cigarettes and weed, and managed to successfully hide the traces of both. I was living a double life. No one at either Target or church knew the real me. It was incredibly lonely. Because of this schedule, I hadn't actually been in a church service in over a year. I was giving and working and leading and had nothing in my world that was uplifting or pouring back into me.

One Sunday, I was finally able to break the cycle. I showed up on a Sunday, albeit slightly hungover so I guess the cycle wasn't totally broken, and a miracle had happened. All of the people who were supposed to teach or lead all of the kids' classes had shown up and no one needed me to cover for them! I was actually able to go sit in a service!

As I sat there, something in the worship really moved me, so I got up and went out to the lobby so that my open weeping didn't disturb anyone else. As I stood in the lobby trying to pull myself together, a woman approached me as she came out of the restroom. I knew this woman well. She was one of my Sunday school teachers and I expected an interaction that included "Are you ok? How can I help?" and a big hug.

What I got was "Hey Meghan, sorry to add this to your plate when it looks like you're stressed, but I'll be out of town next weekend. Can you cover for me?" I was stunned. I heard myself agree to cover for her, but my head felt disconnected from my body, as if I was watching the whole experience instead of living it. I thought, "I'll bet I could go smoke a bowl in the parking lot across the street and no one would care as long as I showed up on time to teach their kids the motions to *It's a Big Big House*." It felt like the only way for me to have a place in church was to earn it through my service and that no one actually cared about me outside of that. It felt like, because I was twenty-six and single and not starting a family like most of the other people at the church my age, that I shouldn't be there if I wasn't doing something.

I left that church that day and I didn't look back. I sent a letter to the elders resigning my position on staff. I quit working with the youth group. I lost a few friends in the process who didn't understand me or what I was talking about. It hurt.

I didn't do church for a year. I didn't even really have anything to do with God at all. I let that part of me sit on the back burner, only to be brought out when it was deemed as necessary for me to go to church with my family for some holiday or another. I was pretty sure God was done with me too. After all, none of the things I had prayed for had worked out. He seemed to be far away and totally deaf to my requests for a better job, or a man, or a magical gift of money so I could move out of my parents' place. In my understanding of God at that point, He was not holding up His end of the bargain. You see, I felt I had been misled. As if God Himself was pulling the ultimate "gotcha" on someone who, up until that point, had been following the *shoulds*.

You see, my take-away based on the way it was presented to me as I was growing up in that youth group culture was this: If you follow the rules and are a "good girl" then you will be rewarded with a super-hot Christian husband, who will probably be a worship leader or a youth pastor, and you will have a perfect marriage with amazing sex and adorable kids quite soon after you graduate from college. Everything had been presented as a tit-for-tat situation and it felt like someone wasn't holding up His end of the deal. I had been a (relatively) good girl, and while I certainly pushed the boundaries on occasion, I still felt like I had done a good enough job to have been given the prize. Like maybe not a worship leader, but I was at least on track for a guy with a good job who taught Sunday school or something. I had done way better than many other girls I knew from youth group and they seemed to have gotten good husbands anyway. I felt duped.

Everything I knew about God to this point was based off of a system of *should* and *should not*. It hit me like a ton of bricks that maybe the "do it my way and you'll get a reward" version of God that I knew, wasn't really who God was at all. All of the sudden it felt like everything I had done, every guy I hadn't let take things any further, anything I had said no to because "I'm a Christian," all the hours I had given in volunteering and serving, all of it felt like it had been for nothing. I knew all along that God was not some magic genie in a bottle who was just there to grant wishes. What I did not understand was who God actually was if He wasn't the person at the other end of the bargaining table. I understood that version of God because it felt like all of the other systems I had thrived in. Do well, follow the rules, get rewarded, repeat. I knew that plan and I thought I was doing a decent enough job at it but there was no reward.

I spent the next year of my life pretty angry. It was clear that the God I thought I knew wasn't who I thought He was at all, and I was pretty sure that I had no interest in getting to know the real one. I was burned out on ministry, I was hurt by the fact that the church had let me get that burnt out, and by the fact that people who claimed to love me didn't bother to follow up or check in after I disappeared from their view. I didn't want any part of what that offered. I was still living at home at the time and my parents saw it. They saw the bitterness and the anger and the fact that on the Sundays that I wasn't working I was sleeping in as a way to avoid any sort of conversation with them about tagging along to their church. On occasion my mom would broach the subject and encourage me to start "church shopping" to see where I might fit, and while I promised to think about it, I did little more than think "maybe next week." I spent more and more time with my work friends, regularly getting more drunk than I should, and through one of those friends met a whole new group of people. People who are still some of my best and closest friends to this day. These were the first people I met who loved me just because I was me, and not because of what I did or didn't do or what I achieved. They taught me what it looks like to be a real friend and to accept people for who they are without trying to change them. Funny how it took leaving the church to find that.

Lesson learned: I should build a foundation of faith not based on the theology of commerce or bargaining with God.

CHAPTER 7

A God Kind of Errand

One night during my year of angry separation from the church, I was at the bar with everyone when I got a phone call. I can now see it was the first of many doors that God used to bring me back to church, back to who He actually was, and to the path He had for me. A former youth group student was calling me, asking me to check in with her parents and see how they were dealing with the fact that she'd gotten an underage DUI.

I knew this student really well and had gotten to know her parents well over the years. I knew that they were members at a church in the North Side of Pittsburgh that had been planted there by the same church I grew up in. The one where I had met the student in question and the one that turned me off of church all together. I knew what I had to do, but I really didn't want to go to this church.

When the church I grew up in, a mostly white, fairly affluent, suburban congregation, decided to plant this church on the

North Side, I was about twelve years old. My whole time growing up at this church, we would do various activities with their congregation. We would have joint services, we would go to help out at events, and our youth group would occasionally do something with theirs. The church was planted by a pastor and his wife who were good friends of my parents, and so my mom quickly got involved in a mentoring program they were running for elementary students. I knew a lot about the church and my mom was very passionate about the work it did in the community. That all sounded just great, but in my mind it would forever be connected to the old church, and I was still pretty angry at them. A few times during my angry year my mom suggested I go down to church there, see their friends, and check it out . out. I blew off the suggestion every time.

This time however, I couldn't blow it off. This student had asked a favor and I needed to help her out. I didn't bother telling my mother why I was going, just that I was, and she was very pleased. That morning I got up, got dressed, and readied myself to go down. By "readied," I mean that in the car on the way there I practiced my "nothing about this makes me want to come back to church, but also I don't want these two people to know that I'm here on a recon mission" apathy face. As soon as I walked into that building, it was clear something else was going on, and my mission was getting pushed to the back burner.

This particular church was in an area of the North Side that most people avoid. It was regularly on the news and it was never for good reasons. But this little church was doing its thing, reaching its neighbors, and bringing hope to a community that felt hopeless and forgotten. For every win, they suffered two losses. For every step forward it felt like they'd take two back.

The day before, on a sunny Saturday, a teenaged boy from the church had been shot and killed while at a graduation party. It was a terrible case of being in the wrong place at the wrong time. I had met the kid myself a few times, and he was always kind, ready with a joke, and put our youth group kids to shame on the basketball court. He was on track to be the first in his family to go to college. He was a shining star in this church and this neighborhood. His mother, brother, and sister were there that morning, surrounded by their church family, as the congregation tried to make sense of the senseless. Tears were streaming down every face. Every heart was broken. And yet, they worshipped. And not just the stand-still-maybe-lift-one-hand kind of music time I was used to. I mean full out, with their whole bodies and all of their grief, still praising God. I stood there, next to the parents of that former youth group kid, and I just watched. I didn't know what else to do. I had never in my life experienced a group of people who had so much faith in the Lord that they were willing to still call Him good in the midst of this unthinkable tragedy. I didn't know what to do. I sang along occasionally, but I found that when I started to sing, I couldn't hold my apathy face. Tears were coming and I really didn't understand it, so I mostly stood frozen and watching. Something in my spirit told me that even if I didn't understand, this is where I belonged. I actually told that to the pastor's wife at the greeting time. With the service not even halfway through, I knew I needed to be there. Later that week I went back to the church for the funeral service of that young man. Yes, as a way to honor his life, but also because I needed to be back there. Something in me needed to be with the community of people at New Hope.

When I'd run into "church people" years later and they'd ask me how I ended up at New Hope, I would often joke that I showed up one morning to run and errand and just never left. It's pretty clear to me now how all of those pieces worked together, and that God had a plan much bigger than I could have ever imagined.

Lesson learned: There is no situation I can find myself in that God cannot use for His purposes.

CHAPTER 8

I Am Not the Axis

When I started attending my new church, I dove in exactly the way I had been raised to. I showed up every Sunday (when I wasn't working my monthly rotation of a Sunday morning shift at Target). I started volunteering with the middle school mentoring program. I joined the worship team. I joined a small group. If the church had an event going on, I was there.

More importantly, I started to get to know the people of the church – people who didn't look like me, people who weren't raised in the suburban bubble I was from. I started to see examples of faith like I had never known and to question some things I'd always believed about God. I did a lot of listening and a lot of learning. It was in that season that I started to learn what "community" actually meant. You can live in the same neighborhood for fifty years and still not be a part of the community. You can attend a church faithfully every Sunday without becoming a part of that community. By the same token, you can live in one neighborhood and be a part of the community in another.

Real community happens when the noun becomes the verb. It happens when there is an action involved instead of just referring to a place. It requires sacrifice, giving of your time, being open to sharing life with other people, and it can be hard, but I've seen the good that comes out of it. In those first months as a part of this new community, I watched lives change because someone took the time to care. I watched my life change because multiple someone's lived out community in action and made me a part of theirs.

I am not ashamed to admit that I stuck my foot in my white-privileged mouth on more than one occasion as I continued to learn what it meant to be in a community with people who were different from me and people from whom I was different. This season of my life taught me one of the best *should not* lessons I have ever learned and it's one I practice daily. It goes like this: I *should not* presume that someone else's lived experience is invalid because it is different than mine. In other words, the world does not use me as its axis. I am not the center.

Here are a few examples of what that looked like. One night at mentoring, I told a kid to not eat so many pretzels at snack time. Then, an older volunteer told me that this boy often filled up because there was nothing waiting for him at home later on. Once I hurried a girl out of the bathroom during Sunday school without seeing that she wasn't trying to be slow, she was just trying to get washed up before church because the water had been turned off at her house the week before. I got annoyed with a student who answered "Allegheny County" when I asked where his dad lived because I thought he was trying to be funny, and to me he may as well have answered "the United States," but what the student meant was the Allegheny County jail. I had never lived in a situation where there wasn't food for me to eat, where I didn't have water every time I turned on the tap, or even in the reality of my parents living in different houses, let alone having one incarcerated. It is human nature to assume that everyone is coming from the same perspective you are. It wasn't until I took a step back and listened to others that I could really start to understand the world in a bigger way.

Once I learned how to look for what was really happening and what was driving these behaviors that seemed odd to me, my first instinct was to run at them with all the "I'm here to help" that I could muster. I believe that most humans are good and that they want to help however they can. In a lot of instances with these students, that meant providing for basics and giving them a safe place to relax, but on occasion it meant I had the opportunity to try and help guide their next steps through high school and beyond. Just as I learned that I shouldn't presume their experiences were like mine, I had to learn that I should not assume that what worked for me and my peers growing up would work for these students. There were so many hurdles these kids faced on a daily basis. So many barriers stood in their way and they just kept going. The flip side of all those hardships was that these kids walked with a faith that I don't think I could have grasped at their age. They had a firm trust that God will provide, and work, and show up, because they had seen Him do it time and time again. It was a deeply rooted faith because they had seen Him prove Himself in a way that I couldn't have imagined when

I was growing up. They'd learned to rely on the only one who wouldn't ever leave, disappoint, fail or hurt them. In my first year at this church, I learned a lot about the things I *shouldn't do* but I learned one giant *should* as well.

Lesson learned: I should always function from a place of assuming that God is in control and should stop trying to take the reins back myself.

CHAPTER 9

An Open Door

It was about a year into my time at New Hope when I started to realize I wanted something different than my job at Target. Spending time with the people of that community and deepening my faith had given me back a confidence that I hadn't felt since college. It opened my eyes to the fact that I was ready to move onto a new chapter. Beyond that, I was also tired of working Sundays and missing church once or twice a month. The age-old question reared its ugly head again though: What does one do with a communication theory degree, especially after this particular one has been out of the communication field for almost four years? I wasn't sure where to even start until I thought about some of my kids at New Hope and their example. At twenty-seven years old, I did a thing that I should have been doing for exactly twenty-seven years. It's a thing I should have done a thousand times before. I sat down and I prayed for God to open a door and for me to have enough faith to walk through it when that happened. I enlisted some of my small group ladies to pray the same thing. Every other time I had to make a large decision about my future, I typically did it on my own accord and asked God to bless it after. As the old joke goes "How do you make God laugh? Make a plan." I had made God laugh a lot, but this time I decided to give the faith route a try.

I prayed. My parents prayed. My church community prayed. After about two weeks, my phone rang. It was the mother of a former youth group student. Her daughter had been in one of my middle school Bible studies and this mom had actually let us host it at their house each week. I had gotten to know her pretty well in that time but I hadn't talked to her in a few years. She called while I was at work and unable to answer, so left me a voicemail. She said, "I'm not sure where you are job-wise right now, but I was talking to an old friend of ours who mentioned a position he's looking to fill and for some reason you popped into my head as the perfect person, so I thought I'd call and let you know about it. Call me back if you're interested and I can give you the details." I must have listened to that message seven times in a row. I couldn't believe it. It felt like God was moving. While in theory that's what I was hoping for, I still don't think I expected it.

When I called her back, she gave me the information. A local private Christian school, whose main offices were on the campus three minutes from my house, was looking for an administrative assistant. She laid out for me the types of things this person would be responsible for and gave me the name of the man to call if I was interested. The role wasn't exactly what I'd had in mind, but part of the prayer was for me to have the courage to walk through doors as they opened, so I called. Two days later I went in for my interview with the Head of School, the Director of Operations, and the campus principal and I left that interview with the weirdest feeling. I knew in my gut that I had done a great job in the interview, and I was proud of that, but I also knew I wasn't going to get this particular job and that was ok.

I can remember sitting in my car being very confused over the feeling. I sent a text to a few of my church prayer warriors and gave them this update. They all agreed to keep praying over the situation. Two days later, the Head of School called me. He said "Meghan, I have to tell you that you didn't get the job. But, I'm wondering if you'd be willing to come back in for another interview. I have been saying that the school needs a marketing and communications person to help me. We really enjoyed meeting you, and by your background I think you may be a good fit for that role. Would you be interested?" Would I? Um, yes! All of the sudden, the feelings in the car after the first interview made sense. I could see God's fingerprints all over this situation and I wondered again, for probably the millionth time at that point, why I had tried for so long to figure out my future for myself when all along I should have been willing to follow what God knew was best. I went for that interview, was offered the job, and accepted it immediately. At the time I thought it was the craziest thing I'd ever seen God do. I had no idea that this would be the first in a long line of doors that I would need the courage to walk through.

Lesson learned: I should not be surprised when God shows up in big ways or provides more than I could ask for.

CHAPTER 10

Taking the Red-Eye to a New Chapter

This exciting new job gave me the chance to do a lot of things. First, I got to tell my church people, my parents, my grandparents, and my extended circles about how God had provided. I closed a chapter of my life. I was thankful for it, it gave me a foundation when I needed one, but I was ready to move on. The first day of the new gig also gave me the opportunity to add a valuable *should not* lesson to my ever-growing list: One *should not* try to start the first day of any new job when one has arrived back in Pittsburgh on the red-eye from Seattle only hours beforehand.

When I initially gave my notice at Target, the timing seemed great. I had already requested a few days off to head to the west coast for a friend's wedding. I would finish my last day at Target on Thursday night, fly to Seattle on Friday, celebrate with them on Saturday, do some fun touristy things Sunday, and then fly home overnight, sleeping on the plane. I'd land, zip home to shower and change, and be all set for my 8:30 start time. The thing is, I am not one of those celebrities who flies first class and has magical potions to make sure they always look hydrated and rested. I was twenty-seven, crunched into a window seat with a man built like a linebacker next to me, and a crying toddler was kicking my chair most of the night. I got home looking like a zombie and not even the cute first-day-of-work outfit I'd picked out was helping. Lesson learned.

This role had been created for me. That meant when the board had approved the budget for the school year, no such line item existed for me. Due to some fancy financial finagling on behalf of the Head of School, it was decided that they had the budget for me to be the part-time Communications Coordinator if I could also be a part-time school secretary for the first year, and then they'd figure out a better plan. This meant that for my first school year, I would come in and be the Communications Coordinator for the first half of the day. I spent those hours overhauling the school's newsletter, emails, website copy, and marketing collateral. I loved every second of it. I had my own office for the first time, and I loved putting on music and getting lost in the creative process of it all. Then after lunch I would go to the school office where I would juggle phone calls, sick kids, envelope stuffing, copy-making, and bus dismissal announcements. I did not love every second of it. Those afternoons were crazy! But handling those afternoons made the mornings possible, so I was there for every chaos-infused moment.

My boss in that role was the Head of School, and to this day, I count him as one of the best professional mentors I could have ever asked for. Not only was he extremely patient and encouraging, but he also taught me what it looks like to lead with equal parts strength and kindness. Up to that point I had worked for bosses who did one or the other, but this was the first time I realized that I didn't have to choose; that it was ok – and even good – to be both. That first year gave me a fantastic foundation in design work, print pieces, campaign structure, and branding, but it also taught me the value of words. No matter what the issue was, my boss used his words in the most impactful way he could. He measured each word carefully and crafted letters and speeches that drove home his point without being too much or not enough. Through all of my college courses I understood the importance of communication, but seeing it in action was a masterclass whose lessons I carry to this day.

Given that this was the first time the school had put a true focus on marketing and communications pieces, it was the perfect time to develop a new logo, color palette, and brand guide. Up to that point, the school had used the academic seal as their logo, but we wanted something that would better capture the feel of the school, its community, and the experience of it. As Head of School, he could very easily have picked a design, set the colors, and moved on and everyone would have had to accept that because of the authority his position held. He wasn't that type of leader though. He understood the power of getting people to buy in. He understood the power of consensus and ownership. He understood that some of the key leaders had been serving this school since its inception and that this was going to be a dramatic shift.

Instead of ruling with an iron fist, he invited key school leadership, the board of directors, and a few key parents to an overnight retreat center where he explained the reasons behind the need for things like logos, colors, taglines, and mottos. He walked everyone through an analysis of all of those things, let everyone have a voice, and brought unity where there had been the potential for division. I left that retreat with all the elements I needed to do my job effectively, but more importantly with a new appreciation for leadership that pushed me to be that kind of leader as I moved throughout my career.

He was also incredibly patient with the randomness during that period of my life. For example, we were due for a long weekend in February one year and I had initially planned to join friends in Punta Cana. When I got back to campus on Tuesday my boss asked me how the Dominican had been, and I replied that "I actually ended up in Virginia Beach for the weekend instead." To me that seemed like a normal turn of events. He still makes fun of the time I meant to go to the Dominican Republic and ended up in Virginia. There was also the time he rolled the punches when I was late to a morning meeting because I had super glued my finger to my shoe in the process of trying to fix it before work. I was on the right track to moving my career along at that point, but clearly my general life skills were still a little out of whack.

Lesson learned: Up until then, experience had taught me that being a leader meant I had to be the loudest and bossiest voice in the room. It turns out it's actually better if I'm just myself.'

CHAPTER 11

Toxic Fumes and Killer Tents

By my second year at the school, I was able to be the Communications Coordinator full time, but I was also asked to take on another task. The upper school Headmaster approached me over the summer and asked if I would be willing to help out there by teaching a Public Speaking course for juniors in the fall semester and seniors in the spring. *Sure, no problem!* Later that year I was asked if I would be willing to help with the school's upper school musical. *Yup, I can do that.* The summer before my third year the Headmaster reappeared and said that Public Speaking was now going to be an every other year course, and so would I be interested in taking on the choir and teaching that class instead, since I'd already worked with a lot of those students in the musical. *Well sure, I guess I can do that. No problem.* Except that I didn't really play piano. I was a mediocre "one finger to plunk out the notes" person at best. Nonetheless, agreed to it. That year

I said yes to helping with the musical again, a larger production this time, as well as to coaching the upper school speech team, and organizing the annual Christian schools speech meet.

It was during this season that I learned another giant *should*: One should address a problem when it arises and not just assume it will go away on its own. In this case, the problem was that my car tried to kill me. For the record all types of killing, or attempted killing, should not be ignored.

At the time, that very cute car that I had bought after college, the one I worked hours at Target to keep in the midst of my mental health struggles, developed a smell. And not a "I left an old smoothie bottle in the car and now it has a bad milk" kind of smell. That kind I was, sadly, familiar with knew how to fix. This smell was something different and I wasn't the only one who noticed. I had been driving the two sons of one of my colleagues to school every morning so they didn't have to wake up as early for the bus. She would drop her boys off at my parents' house where they'd get in my car and away we'd go to the upper school, usually with a Starbucks stop on the way. They definitely started to notice the smell but none of us could place it or find its source.

To this day, if you start to Google "my Jetta smells" the top auto suggestion is "like crayons." It turns out a few specific models of the Jetta had an adhesive glue under the carpet that started to break down after a while and gave off a toxic waxy chemical smell. This was a TERRIBLE smell. It stuck to you. It got to the point where I would drive to school in yoga pants and a hoodie and change when I arrived so I didn't smell like toxic crayons all day. We tried cleaning the carpets. We had the car detailed. Nothing fought off the stench.

While all of this was happening, I noticed that I had been fighting a cough for months, and it wasn't getting any better. After seeing my doctor a few times and noticing no improvement with any of the antibiotics, he sent me for a chest x-ray.

"Meghan, I have some concerning news," he said when he called with the results. "The lining of your lungs is extremely inflamed, but we can also see your spleen in the chest x-ray and that shouldn't be true. Your body is fighting an extreme toxin load and your system can't take much more."

Those are never the words anyone wants to hear. They were scary. They did a bunch of tests to decide what was poisoning my system and it turned out I had a severe allergy to the chemical in the carpet glue that was decomposing in my car. My car was poisoning me. All of the sudden I wished that I had taken my dad up on the offer he had made months ago to take the carpet out and replace the padding to get rid of the smell. I should have. I really should have. I turned him down because I was stubborn and wanted to fix it myself and in the process I almost put myself in the hospital. It turns out enlarged spleens are no joke and it took quite a while for mine to get back to normal.

It was, unfortunately, not my only weird health issue that year. That summer, in my role as Christian school marketer extraordinaire, I spent a lot of my time on the weekends going to community festivals in the area. We would put up a ten by ten tent, pass out balloons and frisbees, and have students come to paint faces. While these kids were being made to look like Batman or a butterfly, I would talk to their parents about the benefits of the school and give them my well-crafted brochure. It was a great plan until we got hit with a microburst storm at one such festival.

I could feel the temperature drop and see a line of clouds in the distance coming in fast, but I had never seen something like that before. Wind and a wall of water came out of nowhere with a force like no other. I was desperately trying to get all of our papers and supplies into the school truck. I had sent the two students running for cover so I was on my own until my boss came back during the deluge. Since we gave out balloons, we needed a helium tank (a very heavy thing by the way) and that's what I was wrestling into the bed of the truck when the tent itself was ripped from the ground and flew at me, an edge of the pole slamming against my head. I stumbled back, leaning on the truck, and started to cry. My head throbbed and I felt dizzy and sick to my stomach. Thankfully, my boss returned at that moment. He took one look at me, a drowned rat by that point, with a growing bump on my head and decided I needed to be taken to the ER. He put me in the truck and off we went. He dropped me off at the front entrance to the ER and went to park the truck. As I walked in, there was a nurse sitting behind the admitting desk.

"Can I help you?" she asked, taking in the mess of a human I looked like by then.

"I got hit in the head with a tent," was all I could manage to get out. My head was killing me, and the lights of the waiting room weren't helping, and I felt like I was going to throw up.

"Do you need to be seen?" she asked.

I looked at her, confusion on my face I'm sure, and uttered what is to this day the snarkiest thing I have ever said to anyone in a service position.

"Do people usually just come here to tell you about their day? Yes. I need to be seen."

Thankfully, she did not hold my sassiness against me, and she got me taken back to be checked out. The blow had given me a concussion and I was told that I wasn't able to drive myself home (which was fine since I had no idea where my car was) and that I needed to be woken up every hour for the first twelve hours, so as to ensure I wasn't in a coma or something. I was still living at home at the time, but my parents were gone for the weekend and my brother wasn't answering his phone, so I called a friend to come meet me at the hospital and take me home.

"Hey," I said when he answered. "I got hit in the head with a tent and I have a concussion so I need you to come pick me up at the emergency room by my parents' house and take me home and stay there to keep waking me up so I don't die."

Recently, when I told him I was putting this story in a book, I asked him if he remembered what he said in response. Neither of us could remember, but to be fair, only one of us had a concussion. We did both agree that it was probably sarcastic. Either way, he came to save the day and called in another friend to help. Between the two of them, I was woken up regularly and have lived to tell the tale. If there is a *should* lesson to be passed on from that whole debacle it is this: You *should* always make sure that the spikes you use to hold a tent to the ground are not the cheap plastic kind and that you have friends who will always make sure you don't die.

Lesson learned: I should always be humble enough to accept help, because I can't fix everything on my own.

CHAPTER 12

The Guilt of No

By the start of my fourth year with the school, my position had expanded to take on some alumni relations and admissions work, and so we upped my title to Director of Communications. I kept the choir and the speech team and said yes to the absurdly ambitious undertaking of getting seventy-five middle and high school students to put up a production of *Fiddler on the Roof*. Yes, seventy-five. I am a glutton for punishment. I even ran sound for the show when our sound guy quit. By the end of that school year, I was beyond burned out. I had been burning the candle at both ends for far too long, while still putting in hours at the church as well.

Actually, my church and community involvement had only grown. That fall, an opportunity presented itself to move into the neighborhood. My family, knowing how badly it had ended the last time I moved out, and that this wasn't the safest of neighborhoods, was not particularly happy with this choice. Some of them were actually pretty hurt, both by the choice itself and by how I handled it. But I was committed to going through doors when God opened them in all areas and this door seemed to be perfect as far as I was concerned. I lived with a friend from church who owned the house and then another roommate our age, who we met through friends at another church on the North Side.

Living in the Frederick Street house was an adventure and a half to be sure. For a girl from the suburbs, it took a bit to get used to things like playing "gunshots or fireworks" or how to parallel park on both sides of our one-way street, but I did get the hang of both things. Living in the city meant that any night sitting on the front porch was an opportunity to meet a wide cast of characters. One night that included a drunk older man, who had just lost his wife of twenty years. One afternoon it was a six-year-old boy who lived down the street who came in the front door on his own because he smelled cookies. There was also the night we stayed hidden inside because I had seen a breaking news alert on Twitter about a "SWAT situation with multiple shooters in the thirty-two hundred block of Frederick Street" and we lived in the thirty-one hundred block. Throughout that fall and winter, I fell even more in love with my neighborhood and the community of people it held, even when that was hard to do.

The following spring, in 2011, I started to wonder if my determination to walk through doors that God opened really meant that I needed to say yes to everything I was asked to do. Knowing what had happened the last time I moved out on my own, I was extra cautious and very aware of my mental health. This time around, I could feel myself getting overwhelmed again.

Not depression-style so much, but just worn out from all I had taken on. The musical was extra hard and drained me beyond measure, all while work and my new responsibilities were bigger than ever, and I'd taken over running the church youth group along with continuing the mentoring program and worship team. When that summer rolled around, I finally had some space to think and relax a little. I spent one evening with a dear friend down by the river looking at the city. I told her how much I loved the summer pace. How much I enjoyed time to relax and just hang out because, the school year frenzy was gone and church programs all took a break.

When I was done talking she said, "Meghan, you do know you're allowed to say 'no' to things, right? Just because you are asked to do something, doesn't mean you have to do it." I stared at her. I had never thought of that. The very idea of saying no flew in the face of how I was raised and sounded like a foreign concept. She continued and said she thought it was great that I was willing to do what God wanted me to do but then she asked me a question that changed my perspective. She asked, "When someone asks you to do something, do you pray about that the way you prayed about the job in the first place?"

It felt like a lightbulb had been turned on in my brain. I had assumed that since God opened the first door that I was obligated to do anything I was asked when it came to that job. It never occurred to me to say no. I spent the rest of that summer praying for the fall. Praying for a clear signal on what I was supposed to be doing and what needed to be left for someone else.

When the school year started that fall, things felt different. I had the communications calendar down pat and the marketing plan was already set in motion. I had said no to teaching and speech team, but yes to the musical. I had made time in my schedule to get back to being in a church small group so that I had time to be a person and not a leader. It all felt good, but it all felt boring. As a way to add something new to the job side, I took the first steps into getting the school on social media. I created a Facebook page and was regularly creating content to engage parents and alumni and getting them to share the posts with their friends to drive new admissions interest. It was fun! Finally, something felt new and exciting again. I had no way to know that taking that step would be the first in a series of career-defining moments.

Lesson learned: I should not continue to say yes to every opportunity out of some misplaced feeling of gratefulness and duty.

CHAPTER 13

The Great Underpants Debate

One sunny Sunday morning I was at church and three teenaged girls that I had never met before came walking in the door. It wasn't unusual for kids to attend that church without their parents. We lived in a neighborhood where parents were not particularly involved, sometimes due to working multiple jobs, sometimes due to drug addictions, you never knew the circumstances, but we were always happy to host their kids. On this particular Sunday, I talked to one of the girls during the greeting time. She introduced herself and said that she was just here to check it out, she said it was the first time she'd ever been inside a church building. I shared with all of them about our youth group that was meeting on Thursday night and invited them to come along. Later that week as we were getting closer to Thursday night, I texted that girl (let's just call her Kid from here on out), invited her again, and told her we'd be thrilled to see her at youth group that week. Much to my surprise, she showed up. Not only did she come on her own, but she also agreed to come with us on a retreat that we were heading on the following weekend.

One of the larger churches in the suburbs of Pittsburgh was taking their high schoolers on a retreat out to a rural part of the state. They had three scholarships available and they wanted to offer them to some of our students, so one of our other leaders, three kids, and I packed into a van and off we went. It was the first time that two of these students, including Kid, had ever left the county. She and I got to know each other pretty well that weekend, and it was amazing to watch someone who had no previous experience with church, or Jesus, or the ways of white youth group kids, take in all that was happening around her.

We were sharing a cabin with a few of the students from the host church and one morning while everyone was getting ready, the girls were having a very heated discussion about underwear. These girls were all thirteen to fifteen years old and came from a fairly affluent school district. The debate was raging over who made the best underwear, Arie or Victoria Secret. I was sitting on my bunk next to Kid and we were just taking the whole scene in. A few minutes into the debate, one of these students tried to engage Kid in the conversation and include her by asking which on she preferred and in the best, "I'm not here for any of this nonsense" tones I've ever heard, said, "I get mine in an eight pack from the Family Dollar and they seem just fine." I was so proud of her! Here she was, in a new environment surrounded by a bunch of people she didn't know who didn't look like her and she unapologetically stood her ground.

After that weekend, Kid became a steady fixture at the Frederick Street house and at church. She'd tag along with me to run errands or come over for dinner or just spend a lazy Saturday hanging out. The more I got to know her, the more I saw what her life was like when she wasn't with me, and the more I knew I had to do something. About a year into our relationship, we got a tipping point where information came to light. In Pennsylvania, youth group leaders are mandated reporters, so I needed to act. I knew that Kid, with her amazing smarts, her fantastic grades, her perfect attendance record, and her desire to do big things needed to have a more stable home environment. Along with some fellow leaders at the church, we made the call to child and family services to report what we knew and they came out to do their due diligence. Unfortunately, our suspicions were correct and they decided that Kid needed a different living situation.

In the city of Pittsburgh we have this awesome program called the Pittsburgh Promise. Students who attend Pittsburgh Public high schools are eligible for college scholarships based on how long they've been in the district, their attendance record, and their grades. Kid had been in the district since kindergarten and was an excellent student. She was on track to receive the highest amount of scholarship available through this program. It was what was going to get her out, because there was obviously no other college fund available. The snag in the plan of finding a new residence for the Kid, was that foster care in this area is county wide and they could not guarantee us that she would be placed somewhere within city limits to maintain her Pittsburgh Promise scholarship eligibility. In a sober moment of clarity and selflessness, her mother put her own wants and needs aside and agreed to let me take temporary custody while she got herself figured out so that we could do what was best for the Kid. All of the sudden, I realized that I was going to go from single, to single mom of a fifteen-year-old overnight.

Lesson learned: I should stop making a five-year plan because whatever God has in store is going to be a crazier ride than I could ever have imagined for myself.

CHAPTER 14

Single to Single Mom

Once that reality set in, I stepped outside and called a dear friend of mine. This particular guy is the best kind of friend someone like me can have, because where I tend to get swept up into emotional decision-making, he stays grounded in fact and reality. It can also be super annoying because he's generally right more than anyone should be and that gets old after a while. Given what it looked like I was about to take on, I gave him a call.

"Hey," I said when he answered the phone. "I think I'm about to take custody of Kid and move her into the house with me and my roommate. What do you think?"

"I think you shouldn't call me and say, 'I think I'm going to be a parent' with the same tone of voice that you had last week when you said, 'I think I want to go get Thai food this weekend."

"Ignore the tone," I said. "Do you think this is a good idea? Am I ready for this? Will I be an ok fake parent?"

"I don't think anyone is ever actually ready to be a real parent, so I don't think there's a good gauge for being a short-term fake one. But I think if anyone can take it on, you can."

That was the vote of confidence I needed, so off I went on my new-found parenting adventure. For the record "If anyone can do it, you can" is the same phrase he has since said to me about changing jobs each time, taking over a company, and writing this book. He's either the best friend ever or he has been systematically setting me up for a series of letdowns just for his own amusement. Knowing him, it really could be either one, but he's also the same friend who picked me up at the emergency room and made sure I didn't die from the tent debacle, so I'm leaning towards the best kind of friend.

Kid moved in with me and my roommates during the summer before the start of her junior year. Early the morning of her first day of school, I woke up to her knocking on my door in tears. She had woken up that morning and had a panic moment over something I took for granted when I was in school, and my heart broke for her. Do you remember back to the first days of school, when teachers would give you papers or index cards to fill out so that they could easily have your name, address, phone number, and parents' contact info all in one place without having to go to the office? I had filled out countless of those papers in my career and never thought twice about them, but Kid woke up in a blind panic because she knew the cards were coming and she wouldn't know what to write. Did she use my address or her mom's? Whose number should she put in case of an emergency? How would she explain it if anyone asked? I was helpless. All I could do is tell her to list me and my address for now and if that changed, she could let them know. Dear Kid, through no fault of her own, was usually so tough, but that day she looked so young. I promised her that morning that I would always be her person, no matter what. I would always be the person that she or a teacher or anyone else could call and I would be there.

Kid eventually did get to go back to her mom's house, but through the rest of high school, I was there. Prom dress shopping, prom itself, marching band festivals and football games, poetry contests, no matter what, I was there. I took her to college visit days and eventually to her college orientation. The day she graduated as salutatorian, I sat in the audience and cried a little when she thanked me in her speech. Ok, I bawled. Whatever. It was beautiful. Throughout her college days, I was a place she'd crash sometimes or the person she'd call after an awesome test or a bad day.

One of the milestones I will never forget was going with her to buy her first car. She was in college and I had been teaching her to drive in my car. After a few rounds of persevering through failed tests, and with some help from a friend of ours who is a way better parallel parker than I am, she passed the test the summer before her junior year. We went car shopping because she was going to have an off-campus job that year and needed a reliable way to get there. Thankfully, my dad is a car guru and we have a lot of friends in the car-selling space, so the three of us trekked to one of their dealerships to buy her car. I was already proud of her for saving the down payment and for her perseverance in the whole process, but nothing spoke to her strength like what happened next.

The dealer she bought that car from was about forty-five minutes north of where we lived and required a thirty minute stretch of highway driving to get home. I had pulled out of the dealership behind her but had stopped for gas, so I was a few minutes behind her getting onto the highway. About ten minutes into my highway drive, I got a call from Kid.

"Hey, I'm on the side of the road. My tire exploded and I can't drive anymore," she said.

"What? Are you serious? Are you ok?" I asked.

"I'm fine but I don't know what to do next," she said.

"Ok, hang on. I'll be there in a few minutes."

I called back to the dealership and talked to our family friend, who was the owner. He jumped in his truck and told me to tell her not to worry. When I pulled up behind her car on the side of the road, it was clear that this was not a tiny hole that had caused a tire to go flat. It was a legit blow out. And it had happened while she was driving sixty-five miles per hour in the left-hand lane. I don't know that I would have been as calm and level-headed as she was about getting over to the side of the road after my brand-new car had just exploded on me the first time I took it on the highway, but there she was, cool as a dang cucumber.

We waited on the side of the highway while the dealership owner came and managed to get the spare on her car. He was kind and gracious and told me to take her home. He would have the car towed back to his shop and replace all the tires free of charge to make sure Kid was safe. Even then, with the craziness of a tire blow out and the disappointment of not getting to take the thing she had worked so hard for home with her that day, Kid was still just rolling with it. Life had taught her repeatedly to not sweat the small stuff and to not let anything rattle you. It had taught her to always keep going. Even now, she is still as tough as nails and always keeps going no matter what obstacle she faces. And through it all, I am still her person and the one she will call if she needs someone to be in her corner.

When it comes to the *shoulds* and *should nots* of my life, there are a lot of situations where I look back and say, "Yeah, I chose the wrong thing there." Kid is not one of those choices. It was not always easy, but there is no doubt in my mind that God orchestrated that whole relationship and that I was meant to step in and be her person. A lot of people thought I should have spent more time weighing out the pros and cons over whether or not I should take on the responsibility, but that was and is one of the surest *shoulds* of my life. It's been a rollercoaster of an adventure, but through all of the ups and downs I learned deep lessons about trusting that God will provide and that He has a plan that's bigger than I know.

Lesson learned: I should always keep an open heart for what God calls me to do, no matter how big or how hard it may seem. If He planned it, I can do it.

CHAPTER 15

Well How About That, Brandon Heath!

When one is in charge of the marketing for a private Christian school, one knows that the best bet for advertising is, in fact, the local Christian radio station. During my time working in this job, I had figured out what kinds of commercials worked best. I had it down to a science. And I had also developed a very good relationship with both the general sales manager as well as our account rep for the Christian radio station. We got together regularly to talk about the upcoming campaigns. One day I was at lunch with the two of them and I was sharing with them some of the things that I had started to do for the school on social media. I talked about how our alumni were sharing posts, our parents were sharing things with their community and with their friends from church. I was very pleased with how it all was going.

The sales manager said, "Meghan that's really interesting. Would you be willing to come into a sales meeting some week and talk to our sales reps about how our other clients might be able to do similar things?" I told him I'd be happy to do that! It sounded like fun to be able to share with people what I had started to learn about this new beast called social media that was taking over the inter-webs.

A few weeks later, I went to the station offices to speak with their sales team. The sales manager was there with his team, all of which I expected. What I did not anticipate was the general manager of the station sitting in the back corner of the room with his arms crossed the whole time. I talked to their team about how I'd set up the school's accounts, the types of content I was posting, and why it was helpful to our overall marketing efforts. I realize sitting here many years later how absurd that statement sounds. Was there ever really a time when every person on the planet didn't know how to set up pages, publish content, and create their own personal brand online? Yes. There was. And it was strangely not that long ago.

Throughout my presentation and the question-and-answer session that followed, the general manager man remained in the corner, arms never uncrossing. He never said anything. He just sat and watched. It kind of made me nervous. I know now that the man in the corner had been running this cluster of radio stations in the Pittsburgh market since it started in the mid-1990s, but he had been in radio since he was eighteen. When I met him that day, he was almost seventy. Radio was his life-long career. The man was a legend in the Christian radio market, but I had no idea about any of that at the time. I only knew him as the crossed-armed skeptic in the corner. Imagine my surprise when a few weeks after the sales meeting, the school secretary buzzed me in my office to tell me that the cross-armed man was on the phone for me.

"Meghan," he said. "I want you to know up front that I really appreciated you coming out to talk with our team. I have some questions about some of the things you said. I was wondering if you would be willing to go to lunch with me sometime and talk about it."

"Sure!" I said, happily agreeing to what I assumed would be a very tasty free lunch. "I'd be happy to do that." And I *was* happy to do it, free lunch aside. I honestly assumed that this man had a lot of the same questions that my grandparents had when I started to talk about these things. "What's a Twitter?" or "Is my face in that book?" That sort of thing. I figured we'd chat about how the internet worked, I'd get a good meal, and then I could pat myself on the back for a job well done being nice to my elders for the day.

The morning of the lunch started out like any other day. I woke up, stopped at the café in my neighborhood to get a coffee and say hello to the kids from church who were waiting for the bus, and I headed to the upper school campus and taught choir class. Knowing that my lunch meeting was halfway between the upper school and my office, I chose to work from the teachers' lounge for a while and then made my way over to the restaurant. On my way I had been on the phone with the admissions director for the school, so I turned down the radio to talk with her. I arrived at the restaurant and was surprised to see not only the general manager at the table, but also the sales manager. I was still working under the assumption that the guys needed a crash course on Social Media 101 and was too embarrassed to admit that to the rest of his staff, so I was genuinely confused when someone else was at the table. Would he really want to ask those kinds of questions in front of one of his employees? It didn't make any sense.

I sat down on the opposite side of the booth from them and after the normal pleasantries were out of the way and lunches had been ordered, the GM looked at me in his very straight-shooter kind of way and said, "Meghan I didn't understand one thing you said the other day, but here's what I know. What you were talking about is the future and we, in the radio world, are already way behind and so are a lot of the people who advertise with us. I'm not sure what it would look like exactly, but if you were to write me a job description that showed how you could help the station do these social medias, but where we could also sell that to the clients as a revenue source for us, we'd hire you to do that job." I was stunned. I had no idea what I said beyond something like "I can totally do that." I had no idea what happened once lunch came or what we talked about over dessert. My mind was racing one thousand miles a minute at the thought of what had just happened.

Even though I was raised in the church and was going to a church at the time whose worship tended to be pretty charismatic, I was not a "signs and wonders" kind of girl. I didn't really believe that God would have enough free time to worry about putting down actual signposts to answer questions. But I do believe that's what He did that day. I fully believe that had I not had the experience I'm about to share, I would have overstayed at the school, repeating the same plans and patterns year after year because I was still so thankful to be working in my field, that it felt ungrateful to dream of anything else. I believe God knew that. I believe He gave me a sign that day in the most tangible way I had ever experienced. Here are two facts you need to know for this story:

1. The name of the school where I was working was Eden Christian Academy.
2. At this point in my life, I was on a pretty big Christian music kick and a new station for that genre had recently come to Pittsburgh. It was regularly on in my car.

I had been on a phone call on my way to lunch, so the radio was turned down. I got in the car, shut the door, and out loud said, "God what just happened in there? Is this for real?" and then took a second to breathe and be still. I then turned the car on, turned up the radio and the first words that flooded out of my speakers where the chorus to a Brandon Heath song that was very popular at the time. The first words I heard were "Feels like I'm leaving Eden." I froze. I made the face that looks like the emoji with giant eyes whose lips disappear. It was a face of shock.

It really did feel like I was leaving Eden. I wish that I could tell you that the sign was all I needed. I wish I could tell you that I went straight home, wrote that job description and never looked back. I wish I was that brave. The truth of the matter was that I had never been so conflicted. I went back and hid in my office that afternoon and I'm pretty sure I accomplished nothing. I let the idea float around in my head for a few days, and that weekend I sat down and started looking at what the station had in the way of social media (not much), what other stations around the country were doing (only marginally better at the time), and at the advertisers on the station's website. I began to map out plans and dream about what could be. I got excited.

That Monday I went to work, taught my students, and had a conversation about the schedule for auditions to the upcoming spring musical. The students couldn't wait and were excited about the show coming up. The woman who directed the shows was already sending me ideas. The spring Admissions Week campaign was also in the works and I had gotten some great feedback about my postcard and print ad campaign for it. For the first time in a while, I was able to see the good sides to what had started to feel like a stagnant existence. I looked around and realized that this nice little life I'd built for myself was pretty ok after all, and it seemed crazy to risk that job and the community I had built there for something so unknown.

When I'd initially been at lunch, the General Manager had even said that this was going to be a pilot program that we were going to try here in Pittsburgh, and that if it was a success, the parent company would look to launch it in other markets. He had said it with a lot of enthusiasm so I expected a better answer to my question of "what happens if it doesn't work?" other than "Well, then after a year we'd let you go." The opportunity presented to me was exciting, but it meant that I would need to leave the job where I finally felt like a success. It would mean not seeing these students and their parents and my fellow staff people every day. It was a risk, and risks were not my thing.

After a few days of this emotional roller coaster, a very wise friend reminded me that taking the first step to something doesn't mean that you have to sign the contract down the line.

She helped me see that I was already twenty-two steps down the road and planning my goodbyes before I'd even taken the steps to write up the plan and see if they liked it. I was steeling myself for my resignation conversation before I'd even heard any information on salary. I was planning for a future that I hadn't even taken the first step towards. She was right and her words are a lesson I still carry with me to this day.

I sat down that night and mapped out a job description, wrote out a proposed plan for packages that the station reps could sell as services, and created a content plan for the station pages. I was really proud of what I'd put together and I somewhere deep inside, I knew this was going to work.

Lesson learned: I should always keep learning. Nothing about social media existed when I went to school, but by using the foundation I had been given, I was able to apply those skills to new platforms and create a career track where one had not existed a few years prior.

CHAPTER 16

One Step at a Time

My plan *did* work. The General Manager and the Vice President both liked the plan and came back with an official job offer very quickly. I was now back to the stay-or-go debate. On one hand, I had reinvented myself and my life during my time at the school. It felt safe. On the other hand, this opportunity had God's fingerprints all over it and I couldn't deny the fact that He seemed to be pushing me through this door He had opened. So many times, in the course of my life I had wondered why I couldn't feel which way God was leading me. In this instance it could not have been any clearer, but I was resisting it with all my might.

When I gave my notice to my boss at the school, I cried. When I told my students I was leaving, I cried. The musical director, my staff friends, some of the parents... yup. Cried. Every time. I had never been a fan of change and here I was forcing it upon myself. It was so hard to leave something that I had come to love.

Thankfully, the team at this radio market was amazing. I knew nothing about radio and they were patient with me. They knew very little about digital marketing, and didn't really see why they needed to learn, but they listened to me anyway. I made some amazing friends in the first few weeks. I also found that there was beauty in a normal schedule. While my job at the school had technically been 8:00-4:30, I taught in the mornings so I was regularly on campus by 7:30 to get ready. I was often there late to help with rehearsals or board meetings or to take photos at basketball and soccer games. I spent a lot of Saturdays doing those things, too. Trying to fit all of that and all of my church work in had burned me out more than I'd realized. All of a sudden, a steady schedule with little to no nights or weekends gave me time not only to do all my church things, but also to have a social life again.

I started at the station in February of 2012 and was told that the goal would be for this new program to go well enough by November that it could be presented to the whole company at their national managers meeting in January. No pressure, just the reputation of the GM and the VP in front of a room of their peers from across the country. So I set out to accomplish the goal. By September that year, the station's social media pages were growing rapidly, and we'd sold enough social media clients to be making money on the idea. Everyone seemed pleased and that January I packed my bags and headed to California to present at the managers meeting.

In my head, I knew that our stations were part of a larger company, but I didn't realize how large until I arrived at the hotel in Calabasas. This meeting was a BIG deal. I arrived on a Tuesday and was scheduled to speak the next day. I don't know that I had ever been that nervous. I gave my presentation. I was stunned at the response. I met the head of the company's web division who knew that something had been happening in Pittsburgh based on our social media numbers but didn't know why. We had a great conversation that week about the future of digital and its impact on the industry, and he's still one of the voices I trust most in this space. I met GMs from other markets who wanted my help in launching the program in their own stations. The whole afternoon was a whirlwind, and when I went back to my room to change for dinner, I called the same friend who had talked me off the ledge and encouraged me to take one step at a time. "Becs, you won't believe how well it went. I'm so excited for what's coming down the line. It's so great!" Then came another pearl of wisdom: Make sure you take the excitement one step at a time too.

I hope it's just human nature and not a "Meghan thing" to jump fifteen steps ahead to the big thing at the end without seeing the little steps you have to take to get there. The wisdom of "just take the first step" felt so wise when it was about making a big decision but felt like it was bursting my bubble on the flip side. The thing was, she was right again. Yes, big things came from that meeting, but it was a little bit like going on a youth group retreat in high school. You get all emotional over this big amazing mountaintop experience that you just had, and you go home fired up and ready to change your whole life. But whether based in fear or excitement, emotions aren't fact. They lose their shine when the work of making big things happen gets hard. She was right both times and I now tried to focus on the reality of each step instead of the emotion of the big picture.

That night, after my speech, and with a little more wisdom and focus, I headed to the company awards dinner. It was exciting to be able to be in the audience when the market I was working for won two awards that evening. It was a great experience to be a part of something so much bigger and I was fighting to not jump back on the excitement train too hard when something unexpected happened. Each year, during the awards dinner, the company has some sort of entertainment. I didn't know that. When the company president got up to introduce the musician, my jaw hit the floor. There I was, in a hotel ballroom full of successful people and really feeling good about myself and my work, and the entertainment for the night was Brandon Heath. He came out and opened his set with that same chorus of "Feels Like I'm leaving Eden" that played in my car when this journey began. It was almost one year to the day since that song had convinced me that this whole thing was really worth considering, and as soon as he started, my eyes filled with tears. It felt like another confirmation that I was exactly where God wanted me to be. All hopes of staying in "take it one step at a time" rational land were gone and I was all aboard the mountaintop high express. I left the hotel the next day to fly home knowing that this trip had started something big and I was ready for it.

Lesson learned: Everything should be taken one step at a time.

CHAPTER 17

Relationships: The Bad Boy

The Bad Boy: Most women do their "bad boy phase" in high school or college. I had mine in my early 30s. At the time, I was living in a neighborhood of Pittsburgh's North Side that was regularly seen on the news for violence, drug issues, and other assorted SWAT situations. I had begun going to a church there a few years before and had fallen in love with the neighborhood and its people. I began running the middle school mentoring program, working with the youth group, and leading worship, and I loved it. Much to a lot of people's confusion, I left the suburbs and moved there to be an even bigger part of the community. As the church and its ministries grew, one of the outreach efforts was to turn a local neighborhood nuisance bar into a coffee and ice cream shop. Another local nonprofit rented the second and third floors of the building from us, and I would regularly see their staff in and out of the café. Enter a bad boy in nice guy clothing.

The Bad Boy was doing work for the nonprofit, helping with their after-school programs for inner-city boys, and I was smitten at first glance. He was cute, he was spending his time working with inner-city kids, and had a snarky sense of humor that I found quite charming. I started finding reasons to email him for questions that I clearly could have googled the answer to, working from the café when I knew he'd be there, and leaving Facebook status messages about my whereabouts to see if he'd show up. Sometimes he did.

As we got to know each other, certain details of his life, his education, and his career didn't seem to add up in the stories he told. I blatantly ignored all voices in my head telling me that these details didn't make sense and he was probably lying. He knew my church friends (who to be fair were skeptical of him at best) but I introduced him to friends outside of church who were very quick to tell me that something was very off about this guy. I ignored them too.

You see I had this picture in my head again of how it *should* be. And to me, *should* looked like this: Date and fall in love with a guy who shares your passion for serving this community. At the time, I already had Kid living with me, and I had talked to the Bad Boy about wanting to maybe do more foster care work down the road. In my head, we would have a cute relationship where we both were doing great work and making a difference in the lives of kids. The thing is, this life in my head blinded me to seeing the truth of the situation.

After a while, the issues became too much to ignore and we parted on not-so-great terms. A few years after the fact, I was switching jobs and needed to do some cellphone number switching, which Bad Boy had helped me set up in the first place back in the day. I reached out to him again via email to see if he could help me solve my problem. He emailed back, solved the problem, and then emails turned into text messages, and texts turned into a phone call, and the next thing I knew I was on my way to spend a weekend in Ohio so we could hang out. It was a picture-perfect late summer weekend full of roller coasters, fireworks, too much tequila, and picturesque views of the lake. The whole way home I let my mind wander thinking, "maybe we both just needed to grow up and find ourselves and now this will work". That weekend was followed by more texts and phone calls, and I was getting excited over the idea that Bad Boy was back in my life. Until he vanished and wasn't.

His job in Ohio was wrapping up at the end of October, and it looked like the plan was for him to return to Pittsburgh. Over Halloween weekend, Bad Boy went dark and I was confused. All of a sudden, his phone was turned off, his social media accounts were deleted, and any email I sent bounced back to me. He had literally vanished, and I once again was left with hurt feelings over the loss of what I thought should have been. For two or three years after that, I would sometimes wonder what happened to him. No matter how much time passed, I still felt that ache like I had lost something and didn't know why. One year, I gave into that feeling when I realized that it was his birthday. I googled him to see if I could find any trace of him. What I found turned my stomach and made me cry.

Bad Boy was currently four years into a nine-year Federal Prison sentence. I read and reread the case files and court documents that I could find online and stared in disbelief. He had disappeared because he was in prison. And not just County lockup. Like, Federal. Prison. For crimes he had committed while we were involved the first time around and that had been happening the whole time since then.

This discovery brought a flood of *should* to my life like I had never known before. I should have listened to my friends the first time. I should have known this was happening. I should have asked more questions when facts didn't add up. I should have found anyone else to help me with the phone thing and I should not have gotten my hopes up again after that Ohio weekend. I should have seen this coming. I should have trusted my gut. I should have known.

This set of *shoulds* knocked me off my game for a minute. Until the day I found out Bad Boy was in prison, I had continued to hold a little hope in the back of my mind that someday, he and I would work out. I felt like he knew me better than anyone and the idea that I could have known so little about him was crushing. It made me distrust my instincts even more. It felt like a game of Chutes and Ladders where I had spent five years successfully moving my way up the ladder towards a place where I was feeling good and confident in myself and my decision-making abilities and then got kicked down the chute hard all the way to the bottom. Into a place where I trusted nothing. The Bad Boy had knocked me down again.

Lesson learned: Grace. Just grace.

CHAPTER 18

Outside the Little Boxes

Since a large part of my radio station job meant handling other companies' social media accounts, I had a lot of client-facing time for the first time in my professional career. I would go out on sales calls with our account executives to try and help them close deals on our services and would spend time with clients working on their strategies. One of my strengths was in relationship building, so I loved meeting new people and bringing them on board with my ideas. In the Clifton Strengths Finder Assessment this skill is called WOO (Winning Others Over) and all three times I have taken this assessment it has come up as my strongest skill. I have always been a people person, so this part of the job was exciting for me until I started to see a pattern in some of those interactions that I have continued to see ever since. It went something like this:

Client (or vendor or prospect): So, Meghan. Are you married? Any kids? What part of town are you in?

Me: Nope! Just me and I live in an under resourced neighborhood in the inner city of Pittsburgh. How about you?

Them: Ah. Interesting. Yes, I am married and we have 2.5 kids and a dog in our house in the suburbs.

Me: That's great! How old are your kids?

Them: Oh, we don't have to talk about that. So about your proposal..."

End scene.

It was as if they didn't know how to talk to me about life outside of work because I didn't fit into the prescribed boxes of "normal." On occasion, it made things awkward with someone who no longer seemed to know how to talk to me like a person, because we had different life situations. Once, I even had a client who called his account manager after I left our strategy meeting and said that he would prefer if I didn't come to these meetings by myself, since I was single and he was married, and even though his assistant and his marketing director were in the room the whole time, he still thought it would be best for someone else from the station to come with me next time. The thing was, his assistant and his marketing director were both men, too. When the account manager told me that he would be coming with me to the next meeting, I remember being so confused. What did this client think was going to happen? If anything, I was a single woman in a room with three men. Shouldn't *I* be the one concerned? Apparently not. Apparently, I held the power to single-handedly destroy all of their marriages by sitting in the same room with all three of them at the same time, so now I needed a chaperone.

In the years that have happened since then, I cannot even count the amount of times that people have said the most absurd things because I am a single woman. Here are a few of the classics that no one would ever say about a single man who was achieving success in his career:

1. I'm surprised they let you travel on business across the country by yourself. Doesn't that make you nervous?
2. I bet you wish you had gotten married when you were younger so that you could have given up all this by now.
3. You're so brave for going into all these meetings by yourself like that.
4. There have to be easier ways for a girl like you to make a good living besides all this travel and long days. That's a lot to take on.
5. I'll be praying for a nice man to come along so you don't have to keep hustling so hard all the time.
6. Do you ever wonder if your success and drive are going to be too much for a man? You don't want them to feel badly that you've done better than them.

I'm not even kidding. Those are word-for-word quotes. I've also been "Billy Graham Ruled" more times than I can count. I mean no disrespect to the man; he was a legend. But I'd like to believe that women and men are capable of sitting in an office or a restaurant discussing business without removing any clothing. Maybe that's just me though.

Those things hurt.

Because my default mode is to please people, when I heard things like this, it felt like there was something wrong with me. Like I had somehow not managed to live up to someone's expectations and that I was a disappointment. Most of these people I didn't even know, and already I felt like I was behind the proverbial eight ball.

I started to realize that I was struggling in the process of living into who God had called me to be, because I was letting their views of who I *should* be define my worth instead. I was, and am for that matter, a single woman who had been gifted by God to love people, to help them tell the story of their work and their organizations, and to lead others well in the process, and I was willing to try to downplay those skills to make others feel more comfortable around me. *What?!* These comments and these expectations had long held too much power in my journey and giving myself permission to not listen to them but to only listen to who the Father says I am has not been easy. But man, when I can do it, it's so worth it.

Women are more than the little boxes people like to put them in. Women are more than a wife and a mom and a job title. Women are more than what they do for other people. Women are awesome. And it's not just me who thinks so. God made us that way and He thinks we're pretty great too. Don't let the voices around us shake our confidence.

Men's words matter and they carry a lot of weight. Regardless of where they stand on the egalitarian verses complementarian debate, the women in life, in offices, and in the world deserve to be able to chase whatever dream they have or live out whatever God has called them to without worrying what the world will think of it. Trust me, we will doubt ourselves enough. We don't need any additional help on that front! But comments and questions that add to those doubts don't do anyone any good.

As I learned to navigate the waters of client relationships in my role with the radio company, I took my biggest steps into learning how to stop using the world's yardstick as a way to define my success as a woman in her thirties. Maybe it went back to that idea of "don't tell me that I can't because, then I for sure will." Maybe it was wisdom that came with moving out of my twenties. Either way, it was one of those lessons I hope to pass on to the students I worked with or younger women coming up the ladder behind me.

Lesson learned: I shouldn't let the opinion of others and their yardsticks for success define my plans or my self-worth. (Yes, I know this is a repeat. It's a hard lesson and I promise it's worth repeating.)

CHAPTER 19

Third Time is the Charm

Over the next year, I helped a number of other markets get up and running with the plan we had built. I spoke on company webinars, flew to other cities to train staff, hosted trainees at our office, and worked hard to keep growing the digital sales at my own station. The social media landscape was changing every day and I was constantly learning. One of my friends from church was also involved in marketing for her dad's company. She and I would often talk about ideas or bounce things off each other. We co-hosted a social media workshop day at a local church, too, and had a great time working on that project. It was fun to be able to connect with someone in the field, doing similar work, who also shared my passion for Urban Ministry.

Eventually, over lunch one day, she broached the idea of me coming to work for her at her dad's company. They were looking to expand their business model and wanted to have a focus on social media. They wanted me to come in and grow a program there the way that I had at the radio station, but they had bigger dreams too. They wanted to see a whole department of social media creators and strategists and for me to run it. The whole idea seemed totally out of the blue. I was gaining traction and success with the radio company and making a name for myself there. There was talk of expanding my role and it felt like it was really just getting started. I left that lunch with her, got back in my car and there was no Brandon Heath song. In fact, the first thing I heard was Oasis's Wonderwall. I assume no one has ever taken life advice from an Oasis song and I certainly wasn't going to be the first. I thought and prayed over that offer for a few days, but it wasn't right. I felt no peace about it at all, so I told her I was sorry but that I was sticking with the radio company. A month or so later, a new offer came from her and her dad and I repeated the process. It took me a little longer this time because there were some things happening at the radio company that made me start to think that my future trajectory wasn't going to be as high or as fast as I'd hoped. I took their second offer a lot more seriously. But after a few days of prayer and weighing the options, I felt led to turn it down again. Not one to be put to the side, they eventually came back with a third offer and made it clear that would be the final one.

As soon as I looked the offer over, I knew I had to take it. Not because the money or the job was so great, but because I just knew. No Brandon Heath needed this time around. It was time to start a new chapter. By that point the general manager who had recruited me to the radio station had just retired and, in a move he still won't let me live down, I walked into the newly appointed General Manager's office on his first official day on the job and handed him my resignation letter. Leaving that company was just as hard as leaving the school. It felt like just as much of a risk to leave a national, well-established organization to go work for a smaller local company. I know it ruffled some feathers. Knowing that I had disappointed some folks was hard for me. Plus, I had made great friends and now I was leaving to start over yet again. I always struggled with change and this time felt even bigger because there were other major changes happening outside of work too.

Lesson learned: Some chapters are shorter than you expect them to be. That's an ok thing.

CHAPTER 20

Church Shopping

Just over a year into my job at the radio company, God had put another giant helping of change on my plate. I'll be honest, I was pretty angry about it. Most of my time outside of work was tied to things at my church. Some of my closest friends were from church and lived in the neighborhood. I was still running mentoring programs and youth group and singing on the worship team. The church's community development arm had bought the nuisance bar on the corner and turned it into a coffee shop where I hung out a lot. I lived in the church bubble and I loved it there. That was, until the founding pastor stepped down and was replaced. Everything changed very quickly. Programs were stopped, the feel of the service shifted, friends stopped attending the church. I was struggling with whether to stay or go amidst the change. Finally, after one Sunday service, I made up my mind. My time at the church was done. And I was mad about it.

That church and its people had changed my life over the course of nearly ten years. It was at that church that I learned what true faith looked like. I learned about true community, the power of prayer, and new depths of empathy and compassion. I learned to trust God in new and deeper ways, and I found a confidence in that relationship that I am ever thankful for. But now what? What was I supposed to do with my time? Where was I supposed to go on Sundays? What was next?

That summer I set about to go "church shopping." I knew I still wanted to be at a church on the North Side. I liked the feel of a smaller community church, but I was open to other options too. Mostly, I just wanted to feel that same sense of "I have to be here" that I felt the first Sunday I'd visited the old church. I was sorely disappointed by what I encountered, and I learned an unexpected lesson about leadership in the process.

Having grown up in the Church all my life, I knew better than to judge any church on a single Sunday experience. Usual pianists got sick so sometimes there were subs. Or the youth pastor was preaching that day. Or there was a women's retreat that weekend and the congregation was mostly tired looking men that morning (yes, that happened). Anything can happen on a Sunday and so I decided that for every church I tried, I would give them three chances. The first Sunday of church shopping I amended my rules to say that I would give them three chances, unless the pastor said something like "The Bible is a nice collection of stories, similar to a large book of Aesop's Fables," from the pulpit. Then it was ok to not give Church One any more tries and move on.

The second Sunday of church shopping, I went to a small local Lutheran church not far from my house. The service was nice, no one said anything heretical, and a few people were kind enough to introduce themselves to me. It actually reminded me a lot of all the Sunday mornings I had spent in Lutheran churches on college choir tours and I liked that memory. I went back the next week and something weird happened. A nice older lady, who had introduced herself to me the week before, came over when I first sat down and said "It's so nice to see you again! I was hoping you'd come back because we've been looking for a new preschool Sunday school teacher." I've never been one to have a good poker face so she must have seen my confusion because she followed it with, "I thought of you since you said you don't have a husband or kids." My face got even more confused. "Just think about it," she said.

I thought about it all right. I thought about it all through church. I thought about it while I walked back home. I told my roommates about it when I got home. I couldn't STOP thinking about it. "Who does this lady think she is?" I asked. It was unfathomable to me that this lady, who didn't know me from a pile of dirt, thought it was ok to ask me to teach pre-school Sunday school when she had no idea if I was good with little kids. What if I had a criminal record? What if I just didn't like kids? And what did my being single have to do with anything? I was fired up. Church Two, I decided, was also not getting a third chance.

The following week, determined to find my rightful place, I went to another local church. Presbyterian this time. Sunday one at Church Three: No one spoke to me at all. Sunday two: Pastor introduced himself and introduced me to a few people. Things were looking up! Sunday three: Pastor greets me and says "I'm so glad you're back. I was talking with the youth pastor and he's looking for another female leader. Would you help us out?" I hadn't told this guy that I had done youth ministry in the past. Again, he didn't know me! But there he was asking me to get involved and lead students. It felt very off-putting!

Church Four was a doozy too. Week one: a few people said hello. Week two: I sat on the end of a row where a very nice husband and wife were sitting with their two kids. He asked if I needed more space and I said I was there by myself. He looked confused, I moved on. Sunday three: I sat in the same row with the same family and the wife said "I heard you singing last week during worship and you have a great voice. You should totally join the choir here! That way you could sit up front with them and not have to be all alone by yourself, because I'm sure that has to be really hard." Yes, for real. It felt, once again, like I didn't belong there. On the card that they wanted visitors to put in the offering plate, along with your usual contact information, were checkboxes under a heading that said "I'd like more information about ..." There were boxes for Children's Ministry, Student Ministry, Family Small Groups, and Seniors Luncheons. It felt like if you didn't fit one of those boxes, then you didn't belong there, and I am a firm believer that no one should ever be made to feel like they don't belong at church. Of all the places, that's where everyone should feel welcomed.

Single people are not always just sitting around waiting for someone to give them something to do so they can stay busy enough to forget their singleness. We have a lot to offer any community just because we're *people* and not because people think we have all the free time. The words that people hear from pastors and congregants should give single people, all people really, a sense that they are welcome and good enough just as they are, without implying that they should have to do anything to earn that place.

After all of these interactions, I took a few weeks off from the hunt and went to a large church on the North Side where my roommates went. It was a nice place to hide for a few weeks but reinforced the idea that a large church was just not for me. While I was there though, I ran into a friend I hadn't seen lately. She was on staff with a large nonprofit that provided a variety of programs to students on the North Side. She asked what I was doing there, and I told her I was church hunting but hadn't found anywhere. Since she knew me well, she asked what I was doing with all the time I used to be at my old church and I shared that I really wasn't sure what to do with it. I missed being in urban ministry, but wasn't sure what that could look like. She had the solution. "Volunteer with us," she said. Within the week I was signed up for a volunteer training, scheduled to help with the gospel choir on Tuesday nights, and committed to teach musical theater at their performing arts academy on Thursday nights. It was awesome. I was back in urban ministry and doing it through things I in which I was gifted and had a passion. Why? Because my friend knew me. She knew my heart, she knew my talents, and she helped me find a place to thrive in those passions.

In my quest to live into who God had made me to be and not what other people think I should do, this interaction was key. Three random strangers thought they knew exactly what they thought I should do, but they made those assumptions without asking me any questions. One friend pointed me in the direction of serving God through the passions and talents He had given me and many years later I am still a committed volunteer. I have loved this program and the kids. I have loved being a part of it! I have loved sharing that passion, getting other people involved, and helping spread the word about their events and fundraisers. Yes, I could have been a fine pre-school Sunday school teacher. I could have helped with youth group or joined their choir. But it made all the difference in the world to have someone say "I know you are good at these things. Would you like to do that?" instead of "I'll assume you can do this, so go do it."

As a leader, I've thought about this lesson for my team as often as I've thought about it for myself. Inviting people to work because they are passionate about it, instead of forcing them to do it because you assume they can, will lead to better results every time. Whenever I forced myself to do something because people thought I should, it ended badly. I needed to put people in positions to do what they are passionate about or called to do.

Lesson learned: As a leader, I never want to be responsible for the bad ending of someone else's should.

CHAPTER 21

So I Sat for a Whole Year

After all of that church hopping and the craziness that went along with it, I went through a year where Sundays became more for sleeping in or lazy brunches instead of for church. In my estimation, I was serving two nights a week in Urban Ministry and there were Bible studies and lessons both nights, so it started to feel like my church quota had been met. Because I grew up in a family so heavily involved in church activities and because that had been my experience with other churches, I had come to assume that was all I really needed. Even the church shopping phase had reinforced the idea church was about what I could offer to aid in its services and activities. Since I was already doing so much service, it felt like taking Sunday mornings off was just fine.

About a year into the season of Sunday brunches and sleeping in, I was in a local bistro in my neighborhood grabbing lunch (not brunch) when I ran into a woman I knew through a mutual friend. We chatted for a few minutes while waiting for our orders. She asked, "Meghan, where are you going to church nowadays?"

I knew that this woman was a pastor and I really didn't want to get into my lack of church with her, so I said I was "between churches" at the moment with a look that said, "please don't judge me." She didn't judge me. She kindly said that if I'd ever like to get back to attending somewhere, she'd be happy to see me at her church any time. I didn't go. I ran into her a few weeks later and she issued the same invitation. A people pleaser by nature, I decided to go visit one week. I went very much in the same frame of mind as when I went to my old church that first Sunday, so I suppose I shouldn't have been surprised when this worked out the same way.

I started attending the church regularly, and a few weeks in, the same pastor asked if she and I could have coffee sometime. I never turn down coffee. So we met up and chatted a little bit about how I was feeling about the church and where my head was about it. She already knew a little bit about my history with churches and I had told her about some of the church shopping nightmares as well. When I said I thought that I would like to make her church my home, she said something that I have never heard come from a pastor before.

"Meghan, I'm glad to hear you think this is a good place for you. We're happy to have you," she said. "But here's the catch. If you decide to make this your home church, I'm putting my foot down and saying that you aren't allowed to do anything there for one year. I don't want you helping out with anything."

I'm sure my face looked as confused as I felt. This was new territory. Someone wanted to have me as part of their church, not for what I could help them do but just because I was me? As that sank in, I started to get choked up. It was the most freeing thing anyone had ever said to me and the feeling was overwhelming. This was a giant step beyond someone knowing what I was good at and helping me find a place to use those skills. This was someone saying, "You belong in the church family just because you are you and not because of what you bring to the table."

That year was profound in my faith journey. At first it was really hard. People would make announcements on Sunday morning asking for volunteers and I'd see a look from across the room telling me to keep my hand down. Even when her husband, who co-pastored the church, was pushing to break the one-year rule to get me on the worship team with him, we held fast to the plan. I spent a year not leading but learning. Not doing, but being. Not running, but sitting. It was refreshing. It changed my entire view of faith and church. I learned more in that one year of just sitting than I had in a lifetime of being busy in the church. For the first time in what felt like my whole life, I didn't have any responsibility on a Sunday morning. When my mind was freed from thinking about the doing, I was able to actually focus on the teaching, engage in worship, and experience church in a new way. I would leave there refreshed and energized for the week instead of feeling like I needed to go home and take a nap.

Most importantly it taught me that I was valuable just because I was a person. I was literally doing nothing to earn a place in that community except existing and everyone was more than fine with it. There is something so refreshing about not having to constantly feel like you need to do more to be valued or loved. I'm sure I should have figured this lesson out a long time before that, but one day during that year I had this lightbulb moment. "This is how God loves me. Not for what I can do but just because I am," I thought. I was sitting in a back row looking around at all of these people that I had come to love, who had come to love me just for me, and it hit me like a ton of bricks and moved me to tears.

When my one year was up, we talked again. She encouraged me to get involved in one thing and make that my thing, and not to fall back into old habits of having to do all the things all the time. I picked singing on the worship team, because that was the thing I realized I missed most. I think a lot of my journey to let go of what I *should* be doing got started in that year. Because for the first time, I realized that all I *should* be worried about doing was what God had called me to be. I learned that my worth as a person was not based on trying to do enough to earn my place. That year, a leader was willing to say, "You as a person are more valuable than just what you bring to the table," was a big part of that change. It gave me a new foundation to stand on in every part of my life, not just at church. It gave me the courage to stand up for what I deserved in multiple areas and led me to a place of confidence in who God had created me to be.

For the first time in my life, it felt like I belonged even if I didn't fit any of the programmatic checkboxes on a welcome card, and it was the most amazing gift.

Lesson learned: One more time, because it takes a while for things to sink in: I shouldn't let the opinion of others and their yardsticks for success define my plans or my self-worth.

CHAPTER 22

Relationships:
Whirlwind; Part One

The Whirlwinds (1 and 2): I am a pro at the whirlwind romance. Not the kind that happens suddenly and lasts forever. Just the suddenly part.

On my second trip to California for the radio company's annual meeting, I decided to go out a day ahead of schedule so that I could enjoy some time on the beach and relax a bit before making another presentation at the conference. My plan was to fly into Santa Barbara, rent a car, spend the night at a cheap hotel by the beach, and then the next day return the car and board the pre-arranged conference shuttle to the swanky hotel they had reserved for the meeting. Nowhere in my plan did I account for the Car Rental Guy.

It is the job of people in service industries to be nice to their customers. The Car Rental Guy (CRG) was more than nice. He was flirty. And I was not accustomed to being flirted with like that. We chatted a little bit, I flirted back, and I managed to score myself an upgrade in the process. He asked me where I was staying and I said out by the beach, which coincidentally was right near where he lived. He said there was a great dessert spot near there and asked if I would want to meet him for some cake later. It's normally at times like this in a story where my close girlfriends say things like, "Please tell me you did not go meet a random stranger for dessert in a city across the country where you know no one," to which I laugh and say, "Of course I did!"

CRG and I had a lovely evening and great conversation over dessert. We walked to the beach and stayed up talking for hours. He asked how long I was staying and if he could see me again and I agreed. I was smitten. I was going to be at the conference for three days and two nights, leaving town on Thursday. Each night CRG came to the resort and picked me up (once with one of my colleagues) and we would spend time playing pool or walking on the beach again. Neither of us wanted the week to end.

On Wednesday night, CRG said I should change my ticket and stay a few more days. It turned out there was snow on the east coast so I would be able to change my flight for free. Much to the confusion of my closest friends and my colleagues, I changed my ticket, found another hotel, and extended my stay by two nights. Everything about that whole week felt like something out of a Nicholas Sparks novel. It felt magical and CRG kept using words like "serendipity" and "kismet." I was hooked.

On the way to the airport on Saturday morning, we decided that our chance encounter had obviously all happened for a reason and that we should keep getting to know each other long-distance and see where it went. I didn't even need the plane to fly me back to Pittsburgh. I was floating on cloud nine the whole way! On Monday when I went back to work, he sent roses to my office. We talked for hours every night for that first long-distance week, even broaching the topic of whether or not I may be able to transfer to a southern California market with the radio company.

Something so intense happening so fast, is often like a flash in the pan, and the fire goes out as fast as it came on. Suddenly, his jealousy issues started creeping in when I was hanging out with my friends or volunteering and unable to talk to him whenever he wanted. Next came news about a teenage kid that had never been mentioned before, who was currently living with an ex-wife I had never heard anything about. Red flags started popping up all over the place, so I had to call it off. We met, went on five dates, discussed me moving my entire life to California, and then broke up all in the span of 15 days. Perhaps I should have listened to all the friends that were saying, "Hey do you think this is maybe a little too much too fast?" More than anything, I wanted to be dating someone and in a relationship. It felt good to have someone pay attention to me like that. I should have known better than to meet up with a random man in a strange city. I should have known better than to let it carry on instead of just ending it after a fun few days. I know I should have done all of those things but it was hard to listen to *should* when *want* gets involved. The best thing I could do was have a circle of people around me, who I trusted to be honest with me, and listened when they saw the situation.

Lesson learned: I should trust the people around me to have my back, even, and maybe especially, when it comes to matters of the heart where my brain can get a little clouded.

CHAPTER 23

Lessons From a Golf Course

All of those church lessons a few chapters back had happened while I was in the first year of working for my new company after leaving the radio station. Once again, I was stepping into a role that had never existed and I got to create the Director of Social media role from scratch. For a company that had always been focused on traditional call center work, this was a big stretch. Regularly, people would stop behind my desk and inform me that I wasn't allowed to be on Facebook or Twitter at work and that if the bosses saw me I'd be in trouble. I tried a few times to explain that those things were my job and that the "bosses" would be angrier if I wasn't on those sites, but that seemed to only complicate matters. It was a big shift to go from a large corporate structure to a family-owned business, especially one that had a lot of "that's the way we've always done it" practices in place. "That's the way we've always done it" is my least favorite phrase.

It gets used to justify ineffective procedures and out-of-date rules and limits creativity. That first year it felt like I was constantly being seen as this big bad rebel because I did things like go on an afternoon coffee run or let my team work from their laptop on the floor if that's where they felt most comfortable. Heck, I worked from the floor regularly myself! It was this company's first foray into having a team of creatives and it was fascinating to watch everyone adjust.

It was during my first two years there that I came to another big leadership revelation: *If it's working, let it be, no matter what anyone else thinks about it.* When I first started building my team, I established our rhythm. A social media or digital marketing team had never existed, so I got to start from scratch building the culture. My friend who had recruited me to the job was extremely encouraging on this front and, over that first year especially, we set out what our values and goals were as a team, we set the structure of our week, and we placed a high value on growth. Every so often I would catch rumblings around the office, where people had complaints about how we were doing things, and at first that drove me crazy. I did not like to have people upset with me! But, the team was continuing to grow, we were driving more new revenue all the time, and we were seeing excellent results for our clients. This thing we were building was working. Seeing that growth and those results gave me the freedom to stop caring about what the office gossips had to say. I no longer cared that they didn't like how we celebrated victories or that we would take team timeouts to do a quick in-office workout, because those types of things meant that my team was getting what they needed to do great work and that was what mattered most.

They say, "if it ain't broke, don't fix it" and that old line gave me a fresh perspective on leadership and management during those first years.

In the same way that my role and responsibilities changed every year back at the Christian school, my role at the company was ever-evolving as well. In four years, I changed titles within this company five times. I was moving up faster than I'd expected. It was amazing to see how God had used my two years at the radio company to give me a better understanding of broadcast ministries and nonprofits, given that those groups were a major client base at the new company. I dove headfirst into serving the nonprofit industry, building new friendships and partnerships and getting to work alongside some outstanding groups. It was a roller-coaster of a few years for the company, with a lot of organizational change and company growth and it was exciting to be a part of it.

I learned a lot of should and should not lessons in my first three years there. For example, one *should* always put nail polish bottles in separate plastic baggies when traveling for business so that one doesn't accidently end up with two fingers nail-polished together when there is no nail polish remover in the toiletry bag. One's boss will have to drive to Target to get some remover. She will not be amused. One should not talk all their friends into helping with a research study on digital fundraising responses, because those friends will regularly share how annoyed they are to still be getting solicitations from these organizations five years later.

On a larger scale, I learned that people have a lot of preconceived notions about who I *should* and *shouldn't* be. Similarly to what I had found in my church shopping days, people didn't know quite what to do with a single woman in her thirties who held a Vice President title. To be fair, it had started when I stepped into roles that started with Director too, but it became a lot more noticeable when those VP letters got introduced. Somehow, going from Director of Strategy and Development to Vice President of Client Services meant that I became more of an anomaly overnight. I once had a man in a prospect meeting ask me if I had any men who reported to me. When I said I did, he asked if I thought they had felt belittled by having a female boss. I said I didn't know, but I certainly hoped my gender wasn't a cause for concern when it came to my leadership. He replied, "Well I know I couldn't do it, that's for sure."

I have had more plenty of well-meaning sixty plus year old men tell me that it's dangerous for a single woman to be traveling by herself on business. One asked me what I would do if my rental car got a flat tire. Another time, a man I had barely met, who was only in his 40s, told me he would wait a few years to do business with our company because, "I like to build lasting relationships and I don't want to just feel comfortable and then have you leave when a man comes along to take you to the life you really want."

All of these exchanges, and the many, many more examples I don't want to even give credence to by writing them down, had an interesting effect on my journey. In almost every other area of my life, I was a people-pleaser and I would shrink myself down as far as it took to make everyone comfortable. These comments did the opposite. It was as if each absurd insinuation that I was somehow less deserving or less capable than a man in the same scenario made me want to work harder, be tougher, and show them exactly what women could do. Their commentary was fuel to my fire and drive and made me into more of a badass. I recognized I had a superpower that drove me to work harder and prove them wrong.

It seems contradictory, but there had always been a "don't tell me I can't" drive behind my "how can I help you" exterior. One time, back in college, I was down in Myrtle Beach with my dad for the weekend. We went out to play Par 3 golf, which was pretty much my least favorite activity, but my dad loves golf in general and quality time makes him happy, so I agreed. (People Pleaser, party of one). I was and am terrible at golf. I don't want to get graphic, but I am a curvy woman who is not built like the female pro golfers. It just doesn't work for me. But out we went to play a round and, as expected, I did not play well. I really did try but my ball always went to the left. In my dad's world, that meant I should spend some time working on my swing and trying to even it out to the center. In my world, it meant that if I just stood and turned to the right, I could get the ball where I wanted it, even though that meant not really being able to see where I was aiming. On the second to last hole my dad said, "This is a tough one. Why don't you just take this one off and let it be?" Immediately my "don't tell me I can't" kicked in and I hit that ball harder than I had all day. So hard in fact, that it whacked off of a tree, flew back towards the green, landed, and rolled into the cup for the only hole-in-one either of us had seen all day. Do NOT tell me I can't. Now, any time I'm explaining to my family why I took a certain action or am pursuing something outlandish, I say, "This is one of those times like the hole-in-one," and they back off and let me go.

I think in my journey of finding who God had called me to be and living into that, it was critical for me to have those experiences where people doubted or questioned me. If everyone assumed I could handle all the things I was being asked to do, I think I would have not been able to go as far or as strong as I did. I think that the four years that I worked for the company were an exercise in proving that it's one thing to meet expectations, but another thing to push yourself beyond them because someone thought you *shouldn't*. The *shouldn'ts* that others used to limit me actually served to propel me forward and beyond. It's a little different of a take on the power of *should* and *shouldn't*, but it was one that formed me into who I am as a woman and a leader, and gave me confidence in those things beyond what I could have ever imagined. It was that confidence that made me say yes to a giant opportunity, even though it churned my stomach again, and how I accidently ended up as the CEO of the company.

Lesson learned: Should not is sometimes more powerful than should.

CHAPTER 24

Here, Have a Company

So how does one accidentally become the CEO? It goes a little something like this: In the spring of 2018, I was at lunch with the former owner of our company and his wife. We had gone off site to talk about a few things including a personnel issue that we are having at the office. As we discussed these things and talked about plans, I brought up the fact that, given that they wanted to retire, it would be a really great time to think about hiring a director of operations or a COO for the company. Essentially, it was time to discuss succession planning. My theory was that this new individual could take some workload off of folks who had too much on their plates and could also start to learn some of the operations that the husband-and-wife duo had run for so long. In my estimation, this is going to be a win-win. It would be a way to solve the personnel issues by eliminating overworked situations, and also give future leadership a time to develop and learn the business. As I explained my theory, both of them sat there nodding in agreement. Then the wife of the pair said, "we absolutely agree. That's what we were thinking, too. But since you're going to own the company, we think you should pick that person."

I had never been more stunned in my entire life.

I'm sure my face looked as confused as I felt. Immediately my head started spinning through a thousand different questions. *What did she say? Did I really hear her right? Am I having a stroke?* None of what was happening made any sense to my brain. I had no interest in owning a company. I certainly didn't have the resources with which to buy a company. Nothing made any sense! Finally, my mouth formed words.

"Since I'm going to what now?" I said. I know, I know, a very well thought out response. I was clearly showing how capable I was for what they were asking. Or not. But in that moment the fact that I could form words at all impressed me.

She looked at me, taking in my shock, and looked at her husband and said, "Did you not talk to her about this?" And he responded with, "I thought I did. Maybe not." He had most definitely not talked to me about this.

"So, what do you think?" she asked.

"I think you know what you pay me and it's not really company-buying-money," I said.

"We have a plan for that, don't worry about it," she said. That seemed like a pretty big detail not to worry about, but this whole thing was so confusing that I just went with it. I figured we'd get to the punchline of this elaborate joke pretty soon anyway, but they both looked very serious.

After a few minutes I finally got my wits about me enough to start to ask a few questions. Once I had a vague understanding of what their plan was, I was told to go and take the rest of the day to think about who I would want to be in this partnership with me. Who did I think was a good person to come alongside to learn the operations and join me in this business venture? What an absurd question! I had never even given thought to who I should be in business with, because I had never planned on being in business. The whole idea was absurd!

I left lunch, drove home, and did the thing I have learned to do when I need to sort out the thoughts in my brain: I went for a very long walk. For me, there had always been something about looking at water that brought me back to a place where I remembered that God was in control. I normally liked for that to be at a beach somewhere, but I live in downtown Pittsburgh and there are no beaches. However, we do have rivers, and I am a giant fan of the trails that went alongside of them. I set out and wandered along the river for a while.

For being May it was still rather cool, but the trees were starting to sprout their spring green buds. We had a storm the day before and as I walked along that stone path I looked at the river rushing by, faster than normal and full of dirt and silt so that it appeared cloudier than usual too. That river felt like me. Or I felt like it, one of the two. Either way things were moving faster than usual. Once I got to the place where all three rivers come together, I took a seat at my favorite spot. Down at that point where the rivers meet is a beautiful fountain and as you make your way from the river and up a few steps towards the park lawn, there are four concrete platforms that sit overlooking the fountain and the rivers beyond it. I have always been partial to having a seat at the second platform from the left and have done my best thinking from there. If there was ever a time for a good thinking spot, this was the day. I thought about the journey that had brought me to that day. I thought about the relationships involved, the people, the places, and the work. I thought about the opportunity before me. I prayed a lot and cried a little. For a few hours I repeated this pattern. I walked, I prayed, I sat and looked at water, I prayed some more, I walked some more, I prayed some more, I looked at water, repeat. Every time I sat and was just still, I heard that voice. "You need to call FBP."

Before I knew it, the sun was starting to set so I started back out of the park at that magical time where everything looks like it is glowing. As I excited the park, with the city skyline in front of me, it felt like stepping out of my safe protected bubble and into a new shinny world. I didn't know exactly how this would all play out, but I knew I was in for an adventure.

At the time, I was thirty-eight years old. If I had learned anything through the course of my thirties it was that God was in control of my career plan and it felt as if I had no choice but to just walk through the doors that He opened. If you had asked that girl in her mid-twenties clearing out the travel size wall at Target where she would be ten years later, there was no possible way that she would have foreseen this kind of future. At some point during my wanderings, I started to think about that girl. It was stunning to me how quickly all of the self-doubt, lack of confidence, and a general sense of inadequacy came rushing back. It felt like everything I had accomplished in that last decade was for nothing. Suddenly, all I could see was how much I was not prepared for what was ahead.

At three separate times during the course of walking and sitting at the fountain platforms while I was praying, I heard a very specific voice in my head. It said you need to call Future Business Partner (FBP). Ignored this voice. I'm not ashamed to tell you that. FBP was someone that I had known for a few years. He was married to a very dear friend of mine, and he was someone whose family I had worked closely with at a nonprofit that I volunteered with regularly. FBP was always the life of the party. But I also knew that FBP was in his early twenties. If I wasn't prepared for what was ahead at thirty-eight, there was no way I figured he was ready at twenty-five.

I did not call FBP that night.

The next morning when I woke up the first thought that entered my brain was, "you need to call FBP." It could not have been clearer. By this point, I decided that ignoring the Holy Spirit was probably not the best way to start out this new adventure. So I sucked it up and I called FBP. That was the Wednesday before Memorial Day weekend of 2018 I called and I said, "Hey, I have no idea what you are doing with your life professionally right now or if you're at all interested, but I may have an opportunity and I really feel like I am supposed to share it with you. Would you mind if we grab lunch or a drink so we can talk about it?" He was gracious and agreed. We got together that Friday afternoon and by July 3, the two of us were business partners who owned a company. I've had some whirlwind romances in my life, but those eight weeks were the wildest ride I had ever been on.

The crazy thing was, FBP didn't know what to expect that day and I had no idea why I had even called him, but God knew. You see, FBP's dad runs that urban ministry organization that I had been volunteering with for years. The one that my friend said would be a great fit for me. That friend, by the way, is also FBP's wife. The whole thing was very full circle. What FBP did know is that he had a vision for building a support center that would help ministries like the one his dad had built. One that could help them with administrative tasks and marketing and fundraising. He had a vision to start this support center from the ground up so that he could help nonprofits who were doing great work. I was about to own a contact center that did all of those things. How God works. It was crazy to me how these pieces seemed to just go together and I quickly got very excited about the idea of what we could build as the next chapter of the company.

Lesson learned: I should never presume to know what God has in store for me next. Never. Ever. I mean, really never.

CHAPTER 25

Me, Moses, and Jonah

A very wise friend had told me at one point not to get too overwhelmed by an opportunity that seemed too big and to just take it one step at a time. You may recall that the same wise friend also told me to take my excitement one step at a time as well. I did neither of those things. In my mind, I could see God working so clearly that I took it as a sign that everything was going to be just fine. I jumped in on blind faith because it seemed like this is what God, and the former owner, and my soon-to-be business partner thought I should do.

Throughout the process, I sat down with a few different people and told them about what was happening to get their counsel. These were trusted confidants. People who knew me well and who I knew would both give me honest opinions and pray for me in the process. All of them were excited for me, but there was also an interesting hesitation each time before they said anything. I chalked that up to the same feeling of confused surprise I felt the first time I heard the news and kept on going. After everything was official and I could tell more people, a lot of the reactions had that same hesitation. I ignored it. I put on the best "this is the most exciting thing ever and I can't wait to get started" face that anyone had ever seen. And then I'd go home, crawl into bed, and cry a lot.

This felt too big. It felt like a giant change and I hated change. It felt like something I wasn't ready for. It felt like the nausea that came with pretending I wanted to be a journalism major but way worse. But the thing was, I read it all wrong. Hindsight being what it is, I can see now that all of those reactions were there because my gut instinct was saying this isn't right. I took it as a sign of not having enough faith to do what God was clearly calling me to do. So instead of listening to my gut and all the people in my life asking if I was sure this is what I wanted, I dug in. I went hard studying the biblical stories of Moses and Jonah. I spent more time on the Minor Prophets than I had in my whole life. I was looking for some sort of inspiration that made me feel like I could do this thing even though I didn't want to or feel brave enough to do it.

We signed the contract to purchase the company on July 31, 2018. I came home that night and three friends came over to pop a bottle of champagne on the roof and celebrate the start of this new adventure. We would tell everyone the next day and introduce FBP to our whole staff. The world was about to change big time, and I didn't think I was ready for just how much. That night kicked off a whirlwind five months of transition, rebranding, and walking the finest of tightropes balancing between respecting the founding owner in his last few months with the company and setting out our vision for the future.

Obviously, I am one who tries not to feel a lot of guilt or regret over things I should or should not have done. This is one experience in my life where I really do regret one specific *should*. I can see that there were more questions I *should* have asked. A lot more. Yes, I knew the business. I understood our market. I had great relationships with our clients and I loved the work that we did. But did those things mean I was ready to leave a role I was doing well in and run the whole thing? The idea was terrifying. Was this what I wanted to do for the rest of my life? Another terrifying thought because, let's be honest here, I didn't know anyone who lay in bed at night as a small child and said, "I can't wait to be the call center owner when I grow up." What I wish I would have asked:

1. What about me and my skill set makes you think that I can shift gears and run this thing?
2. Why now? Why is this process going so quickly?
3. You all understand I'm really NOT a "numbers" person right?

I didn't ask the questions, though. Even knowing by that point how many times God had shown me that following my instinct to get where He wanted me to go was a better plan, I still ignored the churning in my stomach and kept going. It didn't make any sense to me that my gut could be so off base when it seemed like God was opening all the doors Himself and all I had to do was walk through. What I can now say with absolute certainty is that God did open the doors, but I did not walk through correctly.

Lesson learned: It is possible to think I am following God and actually be off course.

CHAPTER 26

A Cloud of Terror

I don't think that anyone ever wants to be a failure. I know I didn't. And I don't even know that I failed necessarily, but I do think I failed to follow what God wanted.

In January of 2019, with the previous owner now officially out of the office and on our own for the first time, I started tackling things like infrastructure, performance management, operations, and budgets. I hate infrastructure, performance management, operations, and budgets. I started spending so much time building spreadsheets and trying to figure out formulas, most of which ended up being wrong anyway, that I didn't have time for any of the things I was good at. My team of digital strategists and content creators saw less and less of me as the things that I was passionate about got pushed to the back burner in my over-packed schedule. I was driving myself crazy. I was driving them crazy. I was working long hours and it was making me into a person I didn't even recognize. Even on the weekends, when I normally would have been hanging out with friends, I was spending most of my time in my apartment by myself trying to recharge. I have d dinner with my family every Sunday night, and during this season, I banned them from even asking about how work was going. As the year went on, I was less and less myself and more and more a shell. I was crabby, emotionally needy, and very snippy with the people closest to me. It wasn't a good phase.

In the beginning of that year, I was invited to be a part of a small summit for leaders who serve the nonprofit industry. Every year they go away to some cool location to dream big about the future of donor relations and nonprofit work. I knew people who had gone, but had never dreamed I'd have been asked. I actually laughed out loud when my invitation came. I felt like I was drowning so hard in my new role that it seemed absolutely absurd that anyone would want my input or thoughts on anything and I felt like I didn't deserve to be a part of that room. I was struggling with some big emotions over all the things and that struggle had led me to believe that I was not the right person for the job. I have been in what I've called the "cloud of terror" … that place where the heavy weight of every decision, coupled with the fear of failure, all underlined by a belief that I was not strong enough or smart enough or capable enough to do all that life demands. These things shook my confidence so much that dealing with personal challenges became even harder than usual too.

When I was talking to friends or coworkers about this invite, I played it off like I was excited. I mean, really who wouldn't be excited about spending a few days at an all-inclusive resort in Mexico being part of a nonprofit think tank? By that point

I was pretty good at feigning excitement and putting on a good front. While part of me was excited to go, I was scared that I wouldn't have anything to contribute and that everyone there would also wonder why I was in this role or at the table. Turns out I was wrong. During those three days I felt connection in a way I hadn't felt in a very long while. I learned from brilliant individuals and I learned that I was not alone in the challenges and fears that I face in my role. I felt heard and seen. I left Mexico with my spirit feeling lighter than it had in months, but like most mountaintop high experiences, the lows that followed those few days felt even lower. Everything just felt too big and too hard. Even my birthday, which I usually love and get totally excited for, felt like too much hassle. I pushed through the next few months literally by God's grace because I had nothing left to offer anyone.

Back in my late twenties I had set a goal to get to all fifty states by the time I was forty. Why fifty by forty? Because the wife of one of my first bosses at the Christian school was doing fifty by fifty and I loved the idea of seeing everythingeverything, but I also do have some overachiever tendencies and I wanted to get it done ten years faster. I was making excellent progress and by the summer of 2019 I only had two states left to go and ten months to get it done. To cross off state forty-nine, I booked an Alaskan cruise with some friends. I was so tired and burned out, I don't really remember the process of getting to Seattle to get on the boat. I know that one of my travelling companions fell down an escalator on our way out of the airport and I know I got to see an old friend from high school the next morning before we left, but if there hadn't been photo proof of that visit I'm not sure I'd have recalled it. I remember spending our first day at sea curled up in deck chairs watching the ocean and pretending to read but mostly just staring and trying to get back to a place where I felt like me again. I journaled a lot on that trip and it was the start to me realizing that something needed to change.

After I got back, I hustled hard through the fall and into our client's busy year-end giving season. It felt like I was in one of those cartoons where a giant dam is about to break. The kind of image where the poor man is standing on one leg with the other foot shoved in one hole but the water is coming out around it and both hands are trying to plug different holes but as soon as one stops another large one starts. It was exhausting! The longer this went on the more, I knew that something had to change, but admitting that seemed like saying "I am not up for the task God called me to do."

The thing was, God never called me to be the CEO.

When I look back on that whole period of negotiations around buying a company, God never said to run it. The former owner said to do that, so I told FBP that's what I should do and we went with it. Plus, it was exciting! It felt good after working hard for so long to have that experience validated. But if I had listened to my gut, I would have seen that I could have taken ownership, kept doing the role and tasks I was best at, and left the operational pieces to someone else who excelled in operations. We all would have had a much better 2019. Thankfully, at the beginning of 2020, some changes were made that forced me to finally have an open conversation about what I wanted to do.

Lesson learned: If what I think God has called me to do is stealing my joy, killing my spirit, and leaving me hopeless, it may be time to reevaluate if this is truly what God has called me to do.

CHAPTER 27

I'm Not Dory. I Couldn't Keep Swimming

At the beginning of March of 2020, my now Business Partner (BP) and I were faced with an operational and infrastructure decision that meant we had to have some very frank discussions about the future. We had gone off-site to discuss it over lunch and, not one to ever beat around the bush, he asked me a question flat out.

"Meg what do you actually want to do? Is this role what you want?" he asked.

Until that moment it had never really occurred to me that I had a choice. Suddenly, I felt like that thirteen-year-old girl back on her first date and the only thing I could think of to do was start crying again. I didn't want that role. I knew I wasn't right for it and I knew it wasn't in the best interest of the company for me to keep it, but I had never realized that I was allowed to say it. There we were, in the middle of a Blaze Pizza, with me sobbing and BP looking like a guy sitting at a table with a crying girl, silently trying to convince other patrons that the tears were not his fault. I was trying to silently assure the rest of the patrons that the scene was not his fault and I was actually fine. It was not my finest moment. It was, however, maybe one of my most honest.

"I hate this."

"Ok. That's a big statement. Tell me more," he said.

"I hate this job. I know I'm supposed to love it and be excited but it's killing me, and I hate it. I don't like the person I have turned into, it's not in my skill sets, and I really think I need to not do it anymore."

Silence.

We both sat there with the giant bomb I had just dropped on the table between us for a moment. I can't say for sure what was going through BP's head. I'm assuming it was something that included some expletives.

Here was my train of thought: *Oh no. Oh no!. I can't believe I just said that out loud. What if that means I'm out of a job? Am I crazy? This is the thing everyone climbs the ladder to get and I'm just going to walk away from it? Oh, this was a giant mistake. I should have shut up and just kept swimming. Dory would have kept swimming. Dory also didn't hate her job with a passion that was making her hate her whole life by association. Or maybe she did and she just forgot. Meghan. Stop. Say something else. And not something about a fish from* Finding Nemo. *Take it back. Say you didn't mean it. Say something!*

After what felt like forever, I said the only thing I could think of to say.

"I'm sorry. I'm so sorry."

"Nothing to be sorry about. I didn't realize how much of a toll this was taking and you clearly need to get into something else, so let's do that. Let's get you in the right seat on the bus so we can all move forward. It's what's best for you and what will be best for the company in the long run."

I'm not sure what I had expected. I don't know if I thought he'd be mad, or hate me, or try to convince me that I could do it, but he did none of those things and it was the best thing he could have done. We talked for a while longer. We made some hard calls. I cried some more. I'd venture to say it was the hardest day of my professional career, but when it all wrapped up and I drove home, I felt a peace like I hadn't felt in months.

Lesson learned: Being honest gives me the freedom to breathe.

CHAPTER 28

Paradise in a Pandemic

It turns out, this momentous decision in my life was not the biggest thing that happened in March of 2020. At the start of the year, I thought the biggest news was going to be that I headed to Hawaii to cross my fiftieth state off my list before my looming fortieth birthday. This giant, life changing conversation happened two days before I was due to be out of the office for twelve days for the trip. The timing equally could not have been worse and couldn't have been a better gift. I needed the break, but there was so much going on that I felt badly leaving in the midst of things. Regardless, I packed my bags and headed out. The friend that took me to the airport is one of my closest people. On our way to the airport we stopped for brunch and over the world's best French toast I told him everything that had happened and that I was stepping out of my role. He'd said it was maybe the smartest thing I'd ever done. As he dropped me off he said, "Do me a favor and come back more like you, ok." And I promised I would. I flew to San Jose to meet up with other friends, and off we went to Kona the next morning.

Hawaii was absolutely amazing. We toured coffee farms, hiked to beautiful beaches, ate amazing food from places with stunning views, and swam with manta rays. After a few days, we hopped islands to Honolulu to experience Pearl Harbor, hike Diamond Head, watch surfers on the north shore, and spend lazy beach time. I had disconnected my email from my phone and was limiting my social media time as much as possible (outside of updating Instagram). I wasn't paying attention to the news at all until I got a text from a friend asking me if I was going to be able to get home. Confused by the question, I jumped on my phone to check see what was happening and I was stunned. The whole world was freaking out and the country was in the middle of preparations to go into a two-week lockdown due to a global pandemic. And I had no idea. Since then, a number of friends had some laughs at my expense.

"I'd scroll through Facebook and it was all 'what about school' and 'the world is ending' and then 'Meghan is climbing a mountain.' The next day everyone was all 'how do I work from home and juggle my kids and why are they closing the liquor stores' and in the middle was 'Here's Meghan at this beautiful beach,'" one explained. Personally, I kind of liked the idea that I could break up the doom and gloom with a little beauty, but I can see where it might come off as a little out of touch.

I was slated to fly back to San Jose on March 14, and from San Jose to Pittsburgh on March 15. Thankfully, I was able to do all of that with no problem, but flying that day was surreal. The world felt so different than it had when I had left the mainland,

and it was a startling reality. I spent the next few weeks in quarantine, working from home like the rest of the world. The difference however, between me and everyone else, was that I wasn't sure what my job was.

I had left for Hawaii after saying that I didn't want my CEO role any longer, but the time frame hadn't given us much time to talk about what I should be doing or what came next. And then the whole world shifted and my team jumped into action and switched us from being a company of people who were all on-site every day to an eighty-five percent remote model in ten days, without my help or input. Not only did the whole world feel different, but all of *life* felt different. BP said the best thing I could do for the moment was to work on getting new business, so I went after that and put all my focus there, but it was so odd to be watching my company run from afar.

In the midst of what felt like chaos, however, I developed a routine that helped me regain my footing. I would wake up and enjoy my coffee while watching *The Today Show*. I'd jump online for our morning team meeting and then get to work on sales and strategy pieces. I'd go out for a walk during lunch to get some fresh air, move, and give my brain a break. I'd come back and make lunch before settling in for the afternoon. I finished work at a normal time and would go for another walk, or do yoga at home, or have a cardio dance party with myself. I read and watched old movies and spent more time in prayer. I started to find myself again. I think the pandemic changed all of us in one way or another, but in my case some of those changes were for the better.

Lesson learned: Rest is actually a good thing and does not mean I have failed.

CHAPTER 29

Relationships: Whirlwind; Part Two

Dating was weird. Dating during a global pandemic was super weird. As a single woman who just turned forty, I could tell you some stories about absurd first dates. In fact, maybe I will. Maybe that will be my next book!

During the COVID-19 outbreak of 2020, I met the Punk Rock Dad on an online dating app. He seemed to be a cool guy; had great taste in music, was an involved father, had recently started a new job. We chatted for a few weeks on the app and then by text and phone calls, because it was a pandemic and you couldn't just rush into meeting people in person. Also, it very much limited what you can actually go do on a date, so it took us a while to make a plan. But we had good chats and I enjoyed getting to know him. It seemed like getting takeout and going to the park was worth the risk. So that's what we did. And the first date was lovely.

He brought me roses, we talked for hours, and it was great. We had that date on a Friday night and we texted back and forth a bit on Saturday. Sunday morning, I woke up to messages about how he missed me, which seemed a little much for someone I had just met, but also kind of sweet. We agreed to do another picnic dinner the next night. Round two was an equal success.

The next day the Punk Rock Dad (PRD) got a serious concussion at work and had to go to the emergency room. I was in a meeting but saw the caller ID come up on my phone as a local hospital, so I excused myself to answer.

"Miss Speer," said the nice nurse, "We have you listed as the emergency contact for PRD. He's sustained a serious concussion and can't drive himself home, so are you able to come and get him?"

I paused.

"Um. Well. I guess I can. I'm about an hour from there right now, so it would take a bit. Can I ask you a question though? Would you be able to give me his home address so I know where to take him, because we've only been on two dates and I have no idea where he lives."

"Two dates?" asked the nurse.

"Two dates," I said.

"You know what? He also gave me the number for his sister. How about I call her instead? And miss, excuse me if I'm overstepping here, but you may want to run away from this one."

"Got it. Ok. Well thanks for calling and for calling his sister," I said and went back to my meeting. She was right. I should have run. But instead, I patiently dealt with a few days of PRD being off of work, bored, and texting me constantly about how much he missed me and how I was the best thing to ever happen to him. It was a lot. At one point I even told him that he was being a little much and that this needed to slow down, and he agreed. That lasted a few hours and then it was right back to constant mushy texts.

On Friday that week, I was scheduled to have the day off so I offered to bring lunch and come over to watch a movie so he would have some company. He said that would be great, and off I went to the eastern suburbs. For a girl originally from the north suburbs, who lived in the city, to go east was a big thing. It was two bridges and a tunnel, which I know may not seem like a lot, but it was one more thing than most people were willing to do. I had an aunt who had lived in Pittsburgh her entire life and had never been to the southern suburbs for precisely that reason. Regardless, I went east and we had a lovely day. Until he ordered pizza for dinner and introduced me to the pizza man as his girlfriend, which sent off all of the "Whoa, slow down dude, this is too much too fast," bells in my head. I went home very quickly after dinner and spent the rest of the night figuring out how to get him to slow down.

All day the next day, I was getting the mushy texts: "Hey baby, miss you," and "I'm so glad I found you," and "I can't wait to see you again soon." All. Day. Long. That night, I went on a walk with my best friend. We were sitting in a park downtown, brainstorming ways that I could politely get him to understand that I needed things to go more slowly, when I got a text that said, "I'm so sorry about this but I've realized that I have a lot going on right now and I'm just not ready for a relationship. I hope you can forgive me." I replied, "Ok," and we moved on with our night.

The next day when I thought about it, I was able to see a whole lot of things I should have seen all along. *Why am I so willing to ignore red flags and justify them in situations like this?* I wondered out loud to myself. I took one of my long walks that day and really thought about that question and here's the answer I came to: I should not be willing to settle or justify behavior just because it feels nice to be wanted. As a single woman, I think it was easy to believe that my standards were just too high or that there was something wrong with me. If I was not personally grounding myself in my identity of who God had made me to be and letting that be the thing that defined me, then I would continue to fall into whirlwinds that left me feeling emotionally spent instead.

I think this was the core root of my relationship with *should*. It was a constant battle, one that I won some days and not so much on others, to be so grounded in my identity in Christ that I can't be swayed by weirdo guys or job titles or transitions. At the end of the day, who God had uniquely equipped me to be was the only thing that should matter.

Lesson learned: Isolation and loneliness will lead to poor choices if I let it. I shouldn't let it.

CHAPTER 30

Climbing Back Down

I climbed the corporate ladder to the top, and then I climbed back down.

The more I thought about the times in my life where I have flourished as a leader and as a person, they were always in spaces where I was living boldly into who God has made me to be. The times that I have been frustrated or dealt with mental health struggles, the times where I have been the least like myself, are when I am trying to live up to someone else's plans or expectations. For the last twenty-five years I can clearly see that pattern emerge and I am thankful for the gift of being able to write about it along with my adventures along the way.

I don't know you, but I know that the same is likely true for you, as well. I do know me. I'm a lot. I'm loyal, creative, and I truly, deeply love people. I am smart, I am a little bossy, and I generally have the attention span of a goldfish unless I am fully passionate about something. Then I am in it for days without remembering to eat. God has given me an ability to relate to people, to get them excited about ideas and plans, to write and create and speak, and to build people up. It's possible that in some companies that skill set is the right CEO, but for our business it isn't. It is however the perfect skill set for someone who someone who is responsible for growing client relationships and strategic partnerships, developing marketing and communication strategies, and building a culture of flourishing. I'm perfect for that job, even if it meant sucking up my pride and moving back down the ladder a rung or two.

If I could make any message from this book stick with you it would be this: God has uniquely gifted you as well and your best self will shine when you are in a space that embraces that. We are not all meant to be leaders and top executives. Some people are and I wish them all of the luck in the world. Some people are called to lead from a few rungs back and I wish all of us the best too. No matter how God has equipped you, I hope you are brave enough to embrace it. There is a world full of people who will tell you what you should and shouldn't do. They will try and influence who you *should* and *shouldn't* be. I'm here to tell you that those people and their opinions don't matter. I wish I had been brave enough to stand my ground the first fifty times that I learned that lesson, but I'm here now, and I am excited to see what comes in the future as I let go of all those *shoulds* and just be who I am created to be. Who God created me to be.

I won't pretend to know what the future holds. I couldn't have ever predicted where the last fifteen years would have taken me so I can't even imagine what's coming down the line for me but I'm excited to see what happens. No matter what the journey holds, I hope I keep all of the lessons I've learned in my head and close to my heart and I hope those lessons encourage you to live out your next chapter with boldness and bravery as well.

Acknowledgements

The journey of this book, from the beginning idea of it all the way through getting it into readers' hands, has been something that I could not have accomplished without the help, support, and encouragement of the people in my circles.

- To Christine and Ken – thank you for the initial idea to start writing, the many walks around the neighborhood to talk out various pieces of it, and for celebrating each step of victory with me.
- To Delia – without your guidance and your understanding of my voice this book would not be what it is. Thank you for all of your work and input.
- To Emily – with our personal history being as old as you are, there is no one else I could have had design the cover. Your thoughtfulness in that process was incredible and I am so grateful.
- To Kasey, Jen, Jan, Josh and Sara – thank you for your feedback and input as advance readers. I am so thankful for your support on that.

- To Stephen and Jeff – your support of every word count update and the overall process of this book means more than you know. I'm grateful you two are always in my corner.
- To my parents, my brother, and all the other cheerleaders who have sent texts or social media comments encouraging the process and sharing the excitement – thank you. Those things mean the world to me.

CPSIA information can be obtained
at www.ICGtesting.com
Printed in the USA
LVHW021414180121
676773LV00005B/470

9 780578 830803